Get Happy or Die Teaching

Languages in English Secondary Schools

by Lalita Vidya Ram

Table of Contents

I dedicate this book to my beloved parents, whom I cannot thank enough for raising me the way they did; for teaching me to be independent and resilient; for teaching me how to make decisions and not to be afraid; for showing me that whatever comes, staying down-to-earth and true to yourself and not forgetting where you come from will always guide you to a better path.

Without the upbringing that I have had, I would have never been able to resist and face the professional challenges that unfolded on different levels and which life has thrown at me ever since I have moved from Germany to the UK.

Without their values and support, I would be nothing.

"Thank you" is not enough. I am forever grateful to you and deeply in your debt for giving me the mind set and the powers that I have as a woman to live the life that I am living today.

The following most certainly applies to me, still.

"Every home is a university and the parents are the teachers."

-Mahatma Gandhi-

Preface

What character traits do you need in order to be a successful secondary school teacher who enjoys their job? Is it being an expert in the subject? Is it the ability to explain well? Is it the pleasure of working with children and teenagers? Ever since I stepped into a secondary school in England, my ideas of how to be a good teacher had to change.

Before I go on, I would like to share some basic background information about myself with you. I was born and raised in Germany, where I completed my education. I'm of Asian background, hence there are two very crucial values I was brought up with. They are respect and dedication. The combination of being an Asian grown up in Germany made me this perfectionist and disciplined person for whom resilience and respect are indispensable. I know it sounds very cliché and prejudiced to say that every German is all about discipline, but it most certainly applies to me. Since my religion is very much about caring for and respecting every creature on earth, too, I could never harm someone nor understand when harm was being done by others. In my teenage years, I had been striving to become a teacher of modern foreign languages. Being able to speak another language always fascinated me and I did well in the subjects in school. In Germany, you have to take two foreign languages. I started helping a classmate in English at first and soon I became the private tutor for other children who went to the same school but were younger than me. Somehow the word spread and also teachers recommended me to parents as a private tutor for their children. Already back then, I felt a sense of fulfilment when I was able to help my private tutees achieve better marks in their French or English tests. So, I decided to become a teacher of French and English for the school type "Gymnasium" which is the equivalent of the British grammar school. In Germany, you follow a different university course depending on which type of school you want to work in. I have always been the kind of person who likes not only to finish a task, but to do it with perfection. This has never been a problem, in fact it always motivated me to do better and helped me to be successful. So, I completed my undergraduate degree and went to France through the ERASMUS programme. During my

Bachelor of Education, I completed a few internships in various schools. I observed the actual teachers delivering their lessons and prepared my own lesson sequences on a given topic for different classes. The feedback was always positive and a confirmation of my career choice.

During my year abroad, I got to know my husband, who was living in England with his family. I decided to move in with him so that we could be together and to make it easier on him as he didn't speak a word of German at that time. We got married and I began to make the effort to pursue my dream of becoming a teacher of languages in my new country of residence.

In this book, I am going to narrate the events from the beginning of my job search until my most recent position. Afterwards, I am elaborating on some of the key factors that shaped my experience.

However, before I start, I would like to say that very soon after I became involved in foreign language education in England, I realised that it is not important how well I could bring across my subject or how well I could get along with the students. The first realisation I made was that generally, Modern Foreign Languages is not a popular subject amongst British students and their parents. "I speak English; why do I need to learn another language?" is the most common comment that you will hear as a language teacher. For me, having grown up and having been educated in a small town in Germany, the school system, work load, teaching methods, and the student mentality in England were a complete shock to my system. I like to believe that teaching in England is a whole new world for someone coming from Germany. To name a few reasons, teachers cannot just come and go to school depending on their timetable. They have to be there before morning registration and can only leave once the school day is finished. Even then, it is not possible to just go home, since teachers have many more responsibilities than just delivering their lessons, which is obvious and applies to every teacher in the world. However, in England, teaching continues long after all the children have gone home. Marking every student's exercise book after a certain number of lessons is part of most school and department policies. There might be extra-curricular activities or subject specific support sessions for students that need supervising. On top of that, there is a huge amount of administrative work that has to be completed, such as replying to e-mails, contacting parents, recording incidents or assessment results on the system, completing forms about particular students' progress in lessons, and so on and so forth. In addition to all of that, there are at least a handful of days where you stay until late for parents' evenings, which are held separately for every year group in most schools. I was not accustomed to this as in Germany, there was only one parents' day on which the parents of all children could book an appointment with the teachers they wanted to see. Also the teachers could directly contact the parents of a student whom they wanted to speak to. If meeting that particular teacher or parent didn't work out, another appointment outside of parents' day would be scheduled. In the English system, teachers also have less flexibility in terms of teaching their subject due to a strict schedule called scheme of work, and very detailed subject specifications for older year groups (KS4 and KS5), provided by various exam boards. Then there is also the, as the British call it, 'Education Watchdog' called Ofsted that supervises and controls schools and teacher performance. Both these concepts exist in the German system, too. However, I'd like to believe that there is still some leeway for the teachers to "do their own thing" and there is a certain trust that teachers can fall back on and work with. Schools in England are rated based on the quality of teaching and student performance, hence teaching and learning is more result-focused rather than happening for the sake of learning, widening horizons and shaping an individual that is intrinsically motivated. As a language teacher, I had to constantly think of ways to motivate the students or to keep them engaged in my lessons, whether through rewards for even a very little matter that they did well or sanctions if they misbehave and disrupt the lesson. Only the minority of children and their parents in England seem to understand the value and see the need of foreign languages and are therefore (intrinsically) motivated to do well or at least pay attention in lessons. Also, because of the rating system, the teachers are checked upon and scrutinized regularly in order to ensure the quality of teaching is maintained. However, everything that I described above is not true for every single school in England, or even London. Each school has different policies, different foci, and a Head Teacher with a Senior Leadership Team that handles things differently.

Bottom line, despite the fact that I already had significant teaching experience before coming to England, I not only had to learn the education system, the staff hierarchy, and that I couldn't sleep in or leave early if I didn't have lessons. I had to learn how to teach all over again.

This sounds all very negative and pessimistic, and maybe dramatic, as if I were trying to criticize or mock the British education system. And honestly speaking, it will be quite overwhelming for someone who was not educated in this system, but in this book, I would just like to share my personal experience during my years of teaching that were a crucial part of my life as they were very eventful and shaped me as a person. I learnt a lot about myself, about how much I can endure and about how teaching, especially Modern Foreign Languages, works in this part of the world. The PGCE (Post Graduate Certificate of Education), which is one way to get into teaching and consists of a university course and several practical placements in schools, and the NQT (Newly Qualified Teacher) year, which is the year in a school after the completion of a teaching course, are an immense learning curve and for me involved sleepless nights, limited time to be with my loved ones, crying like never before, doubting myself, phases of hating children, and wanting to change career paths. It seems that most PGCE students and NQTs go through these rough patches but if these feelings keep resurfacing, there is something that needs to change, but more on that later. If it wasn't for my fellow PGCE students and colleagues in my first school who told me that it will get better and that I'm doing a great job, and for my family who supported me all the way through and kept believing in me, I would have quit right after the second week at my first placement school.

I hope that my experiences will be useful for future teachers, especially from other countries. I don't intend to discourage anybody from becoming a teacher and this book is completely based on personal experience. I just want to tell the world that teaching should come from the heart, that it takes hard work and commitment to become a good teacher, and that teachers deserve all the paid holidays!

1. Calm before the Storm

Do you know that positive feeling that you have when you're innocent and about to start a new chapter in your life? You think "Everything will be fine. I will just apply for a lot of jobs and find one very quickly." So, there I was, innocently looking for jobs in England. At first so confident and thinking that I knew what I was looking for, very soon it became clear to me that I was wrong. I had no clue about the British education system. I only saw words and terms that I had never encountered before. Acronyms such as SEN, SENCo, LSA, TA, KS, and so on and so forth made the letters dance and English seemed like a different language to me. When I eventually found a post where it said 'Teacher of MFL', there were more acronyms and terms that I didn't understand, for example NQT. None of this made sense to me. I didn't know what to look for, or what not to look for and at that time, I didn't know that at some schools you will have to face flying chairs and children carrying knives and others where the parents pay for their child's education and are therefore extremely demanding. But, not to worry, I was just going to arrive in England first and then look for jobs on-location. Of course, that didn't work out the way I wanted either. The job descriptions didn't match my qualifications. Apart from knowing English, German and French and having a Bachelor of Education, I couldn't fulfil any of the other criteria that appeared on the screen. You had to have something called a PGCE certificate, have completed a School Direct or SCITT training, be an NQT or have a certain number of years of teaching experience in the UK. Consequently, I decided to just obtain one of those things and then I was going to be a teacher in no time! After further research, it turned out that the PGCE was the most suitable way of getting into teaching for me, as it is based at a university so that I would obtain some theoretical background and attend training phases in schools. It seemed like a fun course and so I applied for the PGCE for secondary school in the subject German with French at three universities, of which two invited me for an interview after I had also passed the two skills tests, in numeracy and literacy. As only one university in London offered me a place, which I was really happy with anyway, I officially enrolled for the course and prepared myself for the next year. Now, everything was settled. I was going to successfully and as usual without any problems succeed in the one-year university course, as after all, I only had to get a "Pass" in all the assignments, successfully complete the two placements by delivering lessons of a good standard and attending school for a certain number of days. Then I would find a job to complete the NQT year and everything would be fine; except for the fact that it wasn't. I was so relieved to have found a place to obtain that certificate, which I thought would be the most challenging part of the whole thing. Even when friends and relatives of my husband's asked me if I was sure that I was going to do this and told me that I'm really brave, I didn't have the slightest idea of what was ahead. In the meantime, I tutored a girl who wanted to take her German GCSE privately. Again, an acronym; there are way too many! I knew what the GCSEs were from the culture seminars during my studies. I was thinking that the GCSEs were an important exam that the students had to take at the end of Year 11 before they go on to work or do their A-

Levels. What I didn't know was that the GCSEs consist of more than 20 exams for each pupil and that it is almost exclusively the only thing everyone talks about in secondary school and every employer wants to see. I wouldn't find out until working in a school that in some places the preparation for the GCSEs already stars when the children set foot into secondary school. When tutoring that girl, I was still very naive. How should I have known that generally, students in England seem to be more interested in how to pass the exam rather than in learning for the sake of learning? All that mattered was "Will this come up in the exam?" But can you blame them when they know they have to pass more than 20 exams, ideally all of them with flying colours, if they want to do well in their life after school? Naively, I was trying to teach the girl useful phrases and grammar but she kept asking the question above and when the answer was no, she lost interest. Besides, there was little effort from her side to revise or acquire knowledge independently. Eventually, I explained to the parents that there needs to be more initiative from their daughter's side and that otherwise it is a waste of time for all. The parents and the girl, who were lovely people, agreed and decided to pause the German lessons for some time as the priority was to focus on the 'real' GCSEs in school. At that time, I never would have imagined that nearly every student that I would encounter would be merely exam-focused or , even worse, display a careless attitude towards foreign languages. However, what made me think was the family's feedback about my tutoring to my employer. Apparently, I was very competent and very friendly, if not too friendly. It was clear that I didn't have the experience that is needed to teach children in England.

I wouldn't have taken this too seriously, if the mother hadn't been a teacher herself. She must know what she was talking about, I thought. It made me slightly nervous about the course that I was about to start, but I was still very positive and confident that I would have no problems at all. I was eagerly awaiting the first day of my PGCE year.

2. Thrown into cold water

Confidence is key

The first day of university was promising. I was glad to see that I was not the only non-British person wanting to become a teacher. The course, especially MFL, was full of foreigners; mostly continental Europeans. This was reassuring. The introductory speech by the two subject leaders, who were famous in their fields and teaching theory, was less reassuring. After welcoming everybody, telling us what a great university and profession we chose and what wonderful teachers we all will be, they told us this: The PGCE requires hard work and the vast majority of our life for the next year. Basically, there would be no such thing as free time as we would be spending every day planning lessons, writing lesson plans, or writing essays. Some of us would be in really good schools; some of us would be in challenging schools. Some of us would nail a job in the first placement; some of us would need more time to find the right place. Whatever we were going through, the two of them would be there to support us.

Even then, I didn't lose my confidence but kept believing that I would have no hard time at all and that the university tutors are probably blowing everything out of proportion, as is usually the case worldwide. This attitude was about to be seriously challenged. The first day of school arrived quickly. After a month of university with boring lectures and seminars that didn't tell me anything new or insightful, I was very keen to finally put theory into practice and teach those kids some French and German.

Whiteboards everywhere

So, there I was, in a school in outer London, shadowing a student for one day, observing lessons for another few days. It struck me that every classroom had an interactive whiteboard. This is quite sensational for someone who is used to teaching with blackboard and chalk, an overhead projector and student text books. The implications were that the students are used to being taught on the whiteboard and wouldn't engage in any other form of teaching, but also that I would have to learn how to use

PowerPoint for teaching purposes and the teaching software called SMART that was used across all subjects.

Soon enough, I got to know all the MFL teachers and my mentor, who was also Head of Department, for this placement. Maybe this was just my imagination, but I'd like to believe that she seemed a little staggered, if not intimidated, by the fact that I was a native German speaker. In retrospect, this assumption was correct. The reason is the incident that made my confidence crack for the first time. When observing my mentor, Ms A, with a challenging Year 9 German class, she asked me to get some mini whiteboards (again a new kind of resource for me) from the office. I did as I was asked, not knowing that Ms A read through my notes during my absence of not even a minute. Once the students were dismissed and had left the classroom, Ms A asked me to stay back as she had something to ask. Not expecting anything to worry about, I stayed with Ms A but when she asked me what my notes were all about, I realised that there was something she was not happy about. Having read my notes, Ms A thought that I was judging and criticising her teaching and methods. I was shocked that first of all, she had invaded my privacy in my absence and second of all, that she came to such a hasty and negative conclusion about me in the first couple of days. I assured her that my notes were completely neutral and non-judgemental, that I had no right to criticise any of the staff and that I was there to learn from everyone, that all I did was write down what was happening in the lesson. However, Ms A did not seem convinced. Even now, I would stake my life for the fact that Ms A made that exact class part of my timetable and gave me a couple of other difficult classes in order to teach me a lesson. So much about having a good relationship with your mentor, because I could forget about that now. I was on Ms A's radar and there was literally nothing that I could do to impress or please her. Before I had even started teaching my first lesson, I felt disheartened and misunderstood.

Nevertheless, I eagerly planned my first ever lesson on SMART and was very proud of it. It took me hours and hours to create that presentation that covered less than half a lesson, since I had to accustom myself to using PowerPoint for teaching, but I felt prepared and on top of everything. When delivering my activities, the students seemed to be on board and in the feedback, the teacher that I worked with in two classes, Ms H, had good things to say about my teaching, such as that I was trying hard to engage every student and not only the ones that put their hands up. She pointed out what I needed to improve, for example the type of activities and I agreed with that as I didn't have a huge repertoire of tasks to choose from at that time. It seemed like an easy adjustment to make and something quick to learn. It did not take long, though, until that confidence was crushed.

The struggle begins

As the days went by, my workload was increased from delivering starters and half sessions to full one-hour lessons. I found it extremely challenging to plan those at home as I had to think of a variety of activities. Having trained and been schooled in Germany, I found the teaching methods in England rather strange and difficult to adopt. A lot of the teaching was based on games and teaching chunks rather than creating an understanding for the language. I was used to working with a text, having the students do some so-called "think-pair-share", elicit meanings and rules from the students rather than just presenting them stuff on a silver spoon, here the presentation on the whiteboard. It was a completely different approach that I had to adopt and there seemed to be no culture of relying on the students to drive the lesson forward. I had to make sure that the children in front of me were offered a stimulus every second of the lesson and I had to plan for poor behaviour, too. I struggled with structuring a lesson given these circumstances, let alone creating a presentation for every single class that I had to teach. On top of that, I was expected to submit presentations and typed up lesson plans to the respective class teachers 24 hours in advance. When it was Friday, the lessons for Monday had to be ready and submitted. Once, I had sent a lesson to Ms H over the weekend but didn't hear back from her. I became anxious when on Monday – Monday was university day – I still hadn't heard from her, so I emailed her asking if she had received my lesson. The response I received was quite blunt; something along the lines that she also has a lot of other things and work of her own to do and that I couldn't expect her to give me feedback over the weekend. I remember being hurt by the tone of this email and wondering why they couldn't simply have told me in advance and in a friendlier tone that they won't check any emails over the weekend and I should submit lessons for Monday on the Friday before. This added to my stress and I did not cope well with it. Long, sleepless nights at home and tiresome and discouraging days at school were the result. My lessons didn't go well. I was told that there was not enough or no progression in my class and the kids didn't know what they were learning. On top of that, the children were difficult to manage. I didn't know how to approach misbehaviour and rudeness at that time, so if it happened, I would just freeze and let it happen. Obviously, the lesson would fall apart and hearing the feedback afterwards was crushing my confidence even more, especially when Ms A and Ms H rolled their eyes at each other while I sat there completely clueless and disheartened after having heard more and more negative feedback.

Despite all the pushback, I carefully prepared for my first official lesson observation organised by the university, full of hope that I would perform well enough to continue the course. I invested a lot of time planning the lesson to make sure everything was perfect, only to find myself in yet another disaster. The topic I had to teach was the time in French to a Year 8 class. How was I supposed to know that children at the age of 12 and 13 would not be able to read the clock and therefore would never be able to do the time in French? Couldn't I have been warned about this before I miserably failed during my lesson observation? I tried to save the lesson with all my might by completely ignoring the resources I had created and the lesson plan I had written and attempted to improvise and explain the time by drawing on the smartboard. It was hopeless. Just a handful of students cared enough to participate sporadically, but the majority of the class sat there with a blank expression on their faces, either because they genuinely didn't understand ("I don't even know the time in English, Miss" one student said) or because they couldn't care less.

I remember not knowing how to feel when the lesson was over; happy because the time was up, frustrated about how it went, or scared of what was going to happen next? Obviously, the feedback from the observer who was sent by the university wasn't very positive. I could sense that she was trying to wrap her report into kind words, however the message was pretty clear: The lesson was a catastrophe. There are no words for my frustration and anger that overcame me when I thought about the whole matter. Over and over, I thought to myself "Why don't children at that age know how to tell the time in their own language?!", "What are the parents doing at home?", "Why wasn't I made aware of this in advance?!" Pointless thoughts and questions as the damage was done. My disappointment and discouragement reached their peak when in our meeting of that same week, my mentor said to me that things needed to change drastically, that it feels like I am not trying to take any advice on board and that they keep telling me the same things, and this was the worst, that I should think about changing career paths after my first formal observation went quite badly.

It was not until my NQT year, when I realised that it wasn't only me that was doing a bad job. How was I supposed to improve, if all I got was deconstructive criticism and details of all the things that went wrong, but no helpful explanation or frequent modelling of how it has to be or what was expected? I kind of was thrown into cold water and expected to swim immediately. But at that time, by saying all those things, Ms A, for a few hours, dashed my dreams of becoming a teacher and reduced all my hard work for the past three or four years to nothing. She made me feel like I had never felt before in my life, useless, stupid and unable to improve. I can still relate to that feeling after all these years. For me, this was a low point in my life, since in my entire career, my confidence and my self-esteem had never been crushed like this before. Nobody seemed to understand where I was coming from, that I had to adapt to a whole new system, a whole new culture of teaching and methods, a whole new student mentality. I started to think that maybe they were right. How was it possible that I worked so hard every day and night and still wasn't making any progress? Consequently, I dreaded going to school more than ever. On top of all that, the students were still unpleasant and I still didn't know how to handle it. They continuously shouted out, distracted each other, made completely irrelevant comments, and back chatted when I addressed their poor behaviour. In one of my classes, a girl secretly took a picture of me when I was facing the whiteboard.

Ms H caught her and made her delete it. She was given a sanction, too, but I felt a little conscious. What was so funny about me from the back that she had to take a picture of? Did I have something on my back? There was nothing and the girl just thought it would be fun to expose her French teacher. I lost track of what to do and how to behave and there were several days when I went in and just didn't feel that I could become any better, and started to feel exactly as Ms A had suggested, that this job wasn't for me. On top of that, my co-trainee, had a good relationship with her mentor, her lessons were going well and she seemed to be on top of everything. Everybody, including Ms A and Ms H, liked her, they got along with her, she just fit into this group of teachers, who in their free lessons liked to gossip about everything and everyone and also about each other, although they seemed to (pretend?) to like one another. Luckily, there were three people that always made me feel much better during this difficult placement. One of them was a cover supervisor, who would always have an open ear for me in the main staff room. She kept motivating me and said that I was doing a good job and that it is a tough place and a tough profession. The second person was another trainee, who followed a different programme that was school based instead of university based. She was my "gossip friend" and I could vent about my department to her. The third person was a teacher that I only worked with in one Year 12 lesson a week, a young French teacher, whose name I have unfortunately forgotten. It is sad, how sometimes we only remember the negative and traumatising details and forget about the positives. That young teacher assured me that with her class I was doing very well and that I should not lose my confidence or give up my aspiration to become a teacher. With her I could have conversations about things that bothered me, how I was struggling with adapting to a new system and to new methods, as well as behaviour management and she would always have a helpful piece of advice for me.

Getting the hang of it

The October and November months were, in the truest sense of the word, very dark months for me. Not only was I struggling in school, but I also found it difficult to switch off when I was at home and to forget about all that I experienced. It dragged me down and made me feel as if I wasn't allowed to have a free moment to breathe and relax or to do something fun. How could I improve if I didn't keep working constantly? I somehow survived those difficult days, with damage to my self-image, and just before the Christmas holidays, I started to grasp what Ms A and Ms H expected from me. One day, it clicked and I understood how they wanted me to teach. Maybe, I had subconsciously absorbed some of the methods by observing the other teachers or perhaps it was just a coincidence that I did something right. I can't even remember how it even happened, but it just did. After my little but significant light-bulb-moment, Ms A and Ms H became friendlier to me. Since I started making progress and lessons went better, especially with my Year 7 classes, both changed their way of talking to me. I always thought that a mentor or a guide should be encouraging and friendly when the mentee needed it the most; that is, when the mentee is stuck and doesn't know how to come out of this state and step away once the issues are resolved. It seems that some people have different ideas of mentoring and guiding. Anyhow, it started going upwards for me and I held onto little success moments to keep motivating myself. For instance, my lesson structure had improved and the observers were able to see the progression they were talking about all this time. The fact that I was doing something right boosted my confidence so that I began to show more presence in the classroom which the students picked up very quickly. They were more settled and I remember how some of them looked really confused when they saw the "new me" in front of them. Funnily enough, this again made managing low-level disruption easier and I felt more on top of the class. Everything seemed to be finally, slowly but surely, falling into place after a couple of months of struggle and stress. I was very far from mastering all the elements, i.e. a perfect lesson structure, exclusively engaging and varying activities, as well as skilled behaviour management. Yet, I could feel that I was going in the right direction which was also the opinion of Ms A and Ms H. Nevertheless, I was still very nervous about the follow-up observation by my university mentor as the first one didn't go so well, but to my relief it turned out to be a decent lesson this time and even Ms A had some good comments to make. My university mentor, whom I couldn't thank enough for all her support, was always on my side. She believed in me and was always convinced that I was meant to be a teacher.

The remaining weeks flew by and the last day of this placement approached quickly. My last lesson was in one of Ms A's classes. I taught the lesson confidently and I felt like I had done a good job. To my surprise and joy, Ms A felt the same and she even was of the opinion that it was the best lesson that I taught throughout the whole placement. I was over the moon. As advised by my university mentor, I left the school on good terms despite the many tears and insecurity caused. I wrote a thank you card in which I mocked myself as a cry baby and expressed my gratitude to all the members of the department. Although, I felt a little melancholic and emotional when I got into my car and left the staff parking of the school, I was endlessly happy that I didn't have to set foot in this place again... Or so I thought.

3. The sophisticated challenge

La crème de la crème

As the title of this chapter suggests, the challenges in my second placement were of a different nature. My university mentor wanted to spare me from another nerve-wracking experience and placed me in a private grammar school for boys. It was not just a five-minute drive away from home like the first school. I had to be at the train station at 6.30 AM, take two trains and walk for about ten minutes to get to the school in time and back home, which was usually quite late. However, that didn't seem to be a high price to pay for better behaved children, higher standard of teaching and learning, and most of all, the free lunch for staff that would make up for the long journey. So, I was looking forward to beginning my second placement in a much better school. I was so certain that this time, I would do much better and I was going to work in such an environment anyway rather than in a school like my first placement school. You can probably already see where this is going. The problem is, at that time, I was too naïve and maybe a little too arrogant to see for myself. So, I had to learn the hard way that nothing was going to be easy anymore. I had to learn that in England, it doesn't seem to be important how well you can teach according to your own preferences and methods, but how well you can play the game. But I am jumping ahead of myself and I will talk more about my perception of the whole education system in a separate section later on.

The placement started off really smoothly. It was a little bizarre to see only boys everywhere but I got used to that very quickly. If I am being honest, I found it quite nice not to have all the drama with nail polish and uniform skirts that were rolled up so that they became miniskirts.

Everyone in the MFL department was very friendly and welcoming. It was a huge faculty with an impressive variety of languages taught and with some male language teachers, too. Languages are usually a very female-dominated subject. These people were very down-to-earth and seemed to be completely non-judgemental on a personal level, which made me feel very positive. Without even being qualified or having done anything in that department, I could feel a sense of accomplishment. I was mainly going to work with five of the many teachers of MFL. For the first week, I observed lessons in the classes that I was going to take over and was positively surprised by the level of ability. Seeing the really calm lessons (in most classes) and the groups that the teachers taught, I was itching to get started. When I had taught my first few lessons in the following week, I realised that, again, I had to establish myself. Obviously, I had less real behaviour issues in this kind of setting. I never had to do any noise control or play silly games to keep the kids entertained. These kids were a different calibre and they knew they were smart. However, the illusion that I had of grammar schools being completely free from disciplinary problems was soon shattered. It dawned on me that the kids were using their smartness to get away with unnecessary and at times inappropriate comments. It began to irritate me that some of the students thought they could outplay me by making subtle jokes or asking questions that were meant to confuse me and I genuinely began to consider them spoiled and arrogant. I started thinking that this attitude must be the result of having a family with a wealthy background.

My irritation increased when faults were found in every single lesson that I had taught. I again dreaded the feedback sessions as they made me feel as if all my hard work was not enough.

Feedback is a gift

There was one particular teacher, who was extremely encouraging but whose feedback sessions lasted about an hour each time. I understood that he meant well and that he wanted to be as helpful as possible, however these hour-long feedback sessions were rather draining and I felt as if my precious time to work on my lessons for the next day was slipping away. With any teacher, it was not the way feedback was given this time that' brought me down, but the fact that there was not one lesson that I had taught perfectly. Looking back, I think that I probably was a bit big-headed to accept that the way I taught was not perfect to the qualified professionals. In fact, it took me a couple of years to realise that no lesson is ever perfect in the observer's eyes. The reason for that is the system that forces the observer to find an area for improvement, a target in everything they see and everything they do. It hurt me that my methods that were considered excellent and of good practice during my studies and placements back in Germany were now criticized and not good enough. It bothered me and damaged my self-esteem. Another factor that contributed to my frustration and the loss of my self-confidence was the workload. I found myself struggling with having to prepare lessons and lesson plans for the following day and at the same time completing tasks set by the course leaders at university. The teaching hours had jumped from six hours a week in my first placement to twelve hours in this work experience which I found extremely challenging and overwhelming. The final project that was set from university was very time consuming and it was just a pain in the neck. I had been working on this alongside the teaching and the applying for jobs and attending interviews. The end of the tunnel just wasn't in sight. Hours of research in literature, interviews with teachers and other staff, and pages and pages of writing up my findings didn't seem to come to an end. I also had to sacrifice my Easter holidays for this, and this was especially inconvenient as the whole family was on high energy for the preparations for the wedding of one of my brothers-in-law. If you have never seen a Hindu wedding, you won't know how stressful the event is for the couple as well as for their family members. But of course, it's good fun! Not so much in my situation though, where I had to juggle completing this nuisance of a project and welcoming family from everywhere, running errands, eating, breathing and living. It was incredibly stressful but there was no time for complaining as everybody, including my husband, was so busy and in a wedding mood. I somehow managed to finish the project but never before was I so close to the deadline. Can you imagine that I went through all this for a simple "Pass" in the grade transcript? One could argue that in that case, I could have just done the bare minimum, but I think you get me by now; bare minimum is, never was, and never will be an option for me.

Of course, with all this, there was no time for getting ahead with lesson planning and resource making, so when I was back at school, I was more distressed than before. When I spoke to my mentor about my busy Easter holidays and that I spent a lot of time on the project, she merely told me to prioritise and know my limits regarding how much time to spend on university assignments. She went to the same university and had to do the same assignment. According to her, she completed it in a few days so that she could enjoy the holidays. I felt so stupid and helpless. I had never felt this way before and the thought of this stressed me out even more. It was as if things were getting out of control and as if I'd never be able to complete my work to perfection. And this was a crucial factor that contributed to my stress. Being a perfectionist, I have always had extremely high expectations of myself which I fulfilled almost always. Not being able to do anything perfectly during my time as a trainee teacher was beyond dissatisfying for me and had a depressing effect on my mental health. I was completely off balance and I made mistakes that I would have never made under "normal" circumstances. I highly doubted myself and thoughts of whether this is what I really want to do for the rest of my life emerged for the first time. My second formal observation came around and yet again, it didn't go as well as I had hoped. Although the students worked much better this time and really tried very hard, I had to admit that I had missed out an element in the lesson that would have been crucial for the better understanding of the lesson content and the logical progression. There is no way I could exaggerate my frustration and disappointment in myself but this time, too, my university mentor reassured me and backed me up. I wondered how she could not lose all hope and still believe that I would make it. After all, at university, one fellow student after the other was offered a job at their placement school because their performance in their training was so good and met the colleagues' expectations. I was never someone who compared my accomplishments with others' but this got to my head. I felt the pressure to find a position very quickly. So, in addition to the already existing workload, I had to look for teaching positions and apply. My mentor was supportive during my search and when filling in the application forms. Whereas I had thought that I simply update my CV and send it to the schools that had teaching vacancies in my subjects, each school required their own application form to be completed, which turned out to be a tedious job as I had to decompose my CV and fill in all the data into the required fields on the forms. I also found myself writing motivational statements just like on university applications. With the help of my mentor and the teacher who used to give those hour-long feedbacks, I understood what schools wanted to read, which was what I bring to the school and more importantly, why I chose this particular school and why I am so endlessly excited about working at this school, even if I was not that much into it. Back then, I did not realise that a huge part of the profession would be to know how to toe the line.

The future is around the corner

Having sent off a couple of applications approved by my mentor, I felt confident and had the feeling that I had done something useful. I had taken a step towards securing my first teaching position and it wouldn't be long until I would be successful – I thought. Towards the end of the second placement, which is the main and last one of the PGCE, I attended two job interviews. I was over the moon when I was invited to my very first one. It was a school in Dorking and they had called me to verify that I am still available and would send further information with a schedule to my email address. I carried on throughout the rest of the day with a big smile on my face. Now that I had been invited for an interview, I thought that performing well and convincing the interviewers of my abilities would be child's play for me. Again, you see where this is heading and I won't blame you if you think "What an arrogant and naïve woman!" However, this time my illusion of landing a job after the very first attempt was dispelled quite quickly when I saw the email from the school, entailing the programme for the day and the things that I had to do. Not only did I have to prepare a lesson and present myself to the interviewers and skilfully answer all their tricky questions. I actually had to teach the lesson that I had to prepare. I was given the topic, the year group and the class size and it was up to me to draft a lesson plan with resources that would entertain and teach a class of students that I had never seen before in a school that I had never set foot in. While my confidence was at its peak when I received the phone call, it was now on the opposite side of the scale. How was I going to prepare a lesson and also teach it in front of a bunch of unfamiliar kids when I have already been struggling to please my mentor and colleagues in schools that I have observed and taught in for a while, and they were not even planning on hiring me?! When I raised this with my mentor, she basically told me to get used to this because this is how teaching interviews are done in England. So, I pulled my act together and started preparing for the big first interview. Again, this meant sleepless nights, anxiety and stress before the interview day but I was determined to do well. I had my resources and lesson plan checked by a friend of mine, whom I got to know when I started the course and who taught the same languages as I did. She was one of the people who kept believing in me and who was always ready to help when I needed support, academically as well as mentally. She is a good soul and was also lucky enough to enjoy both her placements and to be offered a position at her first placement school, where she has been working ever since.

After some twisting and tweaking according to my friend's advice, my lesson plan and resources were ready and I was waiting for the interview to be over. What I did not know at that time was that it wasn't going to be over for quite some time as this first interview was the first episode of a series of unsuccessful interviews. Being turned down was quite devastating and it didn't help that supposedly I was very close to getting the job, if there hadn't been a more experienced candidate. All I could think about was how close I was to securing a job and then failed. I attended a few more interviews during the placement and was dismissed for the same reason, lack of experience. Apparently, in all interviews, according to the interviewers, I did extremely well and was very impressive but they just had to go with the candidate who had been teaching for several years. It got all the more frustrating when the placement and with that the PGCE course came to an end I still hadn't been able to find a teaching job for September unlike most of my course mates. Although the end of the placement and the course were very positive, I had this growing fear in the back of my mind that I wouldn't find a job at all. Secretly, I made it my goal to secure a post before the graduation ceremony in July. The end of the second placement came with a few annoyances such as having to make up for the extra week of half-term holiday since it was a grammar school and all the days that I had to take off due to sickness and other personal matters that were going on in my life parallel to this draining and confidence-wracking course. Do you remember how in the chapter about my first placement I said that I left the staff parking with a smile on my face because I would never have to return? Well, guess what: my university mentor made me get in touch with my "ex-colleagues" from that school and arrange a few hours to just help out with some classes. To my surprise, the response from Ms A to my email was very positive which made the whole idea a bit less appalling for me. When I pulled up in the parking lot, I realised how uncomfortable I was coming back to this place but I didn't have a choice if I wanted to pass this PGCE. I had been given some information on what class I'd be assisting with, so I made my way up to the IT room where I was supposed to go. To be honest, it was quite startling that Ms H welcomed me with a huge smile and a hug. As you know, I had ended that first placement on good terms with a card, flowers and an overly positive speech but a hearty welcome like this was the last that I had expected and it threw me off. I didn't know how to behave during these couple of hours and the next day and whilst I was still working it out, Ms H delivered some news that I gladly received with open arms. Ms A texted Ms H (as she had already left school) that I could just make myself scarce and use my time more usefully and that they would cover up for me. They didn't have to tell me that twice. Not only did Ms H and Ms A give me some of my precious time back, but also, they were going to pretend that I had been there to make up for my missed days so that I wouldn't be in trouble with university and still passed my course. I thanked Ms H, told her to say hi to Ms A from me and as quick as the wind, I was out of that building and this time, I was definitely not going to return. So, the next day, thanks to Ms A and Ms H, I was able to dedicate more time to my job hunt.

4. My temporary job

After having more or less successfully survived the second placement, it was just a matter of attending university for a couple of days to finish off this nightmare of a PGCE course! Although I was happy that this 9-month horror was over, I didn't feel like I had accomplished anything. It felt more like having scraped a pass (the only "grade" that you can achieve in the PGCE is a Pass) that I didn't even deserve. The fact that quite a few in my class already had landed a job made my frustration and my feeling of being a failure worse. The good thing about this is that it seemed like I was not a person who just bathes in self-pity and accepts the situation. I say "seemed like" because as mentioned previously, I never had to face such a state in which I thought I was failing. Up to the PGCE, everything that I attempted I succeeded in. So, if the PGCE taught me one thing, it was that I am stronger than I knew and that I have strong will-power. With this new realisation, I made it my temporary full-time job to fill in tedious teaching staff application forms and attend those dreadful interviews. After five years, I don't remember every exact interview that I went to but what I do remember is that I felt like I was in a battle. With each audition, I declined in confidence, motivation, and physical strength to put up with all this stress. It came to a point where I was just happy when they called me to let me know that I didn't make it so that I could just leave that one behind me. Throughout the marathon of a total of eight interviews, my university mentor was still supporting me via email. She would say "If they didn't want you, you don't want them. Something better and more suitable is waiting for you." Sometimes, I was happy that I didn't make it into that school as it was too far away or because I didn't like the surroundings and the atmosphere anyways. At the same time, I was wondering if I should be picky like this when it seemed far-fetched that I would land a position at all. However, I was told that if you didn't feel comfortable in a school, you probably shouldn't work there. I remember one boys' school that I went to struck me as disconcerting right at the entrance. The premises were surrounded by huge iron gates with a security system, there were boys standing in the corridors facing the wall and staff that showed me around the school and looked after us on the interview day made those suspicious comments about the behaviour and the general climate in the school. In addition to that, since the moment I had entered the building, I just couldn't shake off that feeling of not belonging and wanting to turn around and leave. And that's exactly what I did. Before I even taught my lesson, I told the Deputy Headmaster, who was in charge of the interview procedure that day, that I didn't want to waste anyone's time and that I sensed that this wasn't the right place for me. It took me a couple of hours until I made up my mind and went to tell him that. I was all sweaty and nervous about doing this and I even discussed this with other candidates. The thought of quitting before even trying made my stomach turn and you can probably imagine how this affected my view on myself. However, this again taught me something, which is that I don't have to force myself to do something I am not comfortable with. If there were going to be other opportunities and possibilities, they would just feel right (I know it sounds cheesy but it's true!). And this opportunity presented itself at my eighth interview. It was a school just outside of London. I went there on a sunny day and already the receptionist was so welcoming that I thought "Okay, maybe this is it!" But of course, I kept my expectations low; actually, I didn't have any expectations at all anymore, although the general ambience was quite pleasant. I began to like the place when I and the other candidates were given the tour of the school and I was torn between not getting too excited and expecting yet another failure. During my tour, one of the candidates was already teaching his lesson. When we passed the classroom that he was in, the candidate was just about to send a student outside. Now, I wasn't sure if this would have an impact on him being appointed, but I knew that this wasn't a good position to be in, having to get rid of a student, during an interview. Back in the staff room, we were just chatting amongst ourselves and to my convenience it turned out that one of my "rivals" was not even a real candidate, but was going to start a school-based teacher training there. She was so kind to let us know that she was not after the position that we had applied for. At this point, I had my hopes at such an altitude that it would hurt rather badly should I not be selected for this post. A few minutes later, I and the other "real" candidate were called to teach our lessons simultaneously and it just amused me that unlike me, she had not made the printing and photo copying that she needed for her lesson beforehand but asked the teacher who was organising the interview day to do it for her. This time I knew that this did not make a good impression and my confidence rose. Like many of my other interview lessons, this one went smoothly and I was quite happy with myself, but we know that this didn't mean anything. I had to wait until I had completed the individual interview with the Head of Department, the Deputy Head teacher, and the Head teacher. Even after that, I still felt positive about the whole day and I left the school thinking that if I didn't make it this time again, with things going wrong for the other candidates and almost everything going right for me, then I was clearly too stupid for all this. Also, most likely, it would have been my last shot for that year as it was the end of June and already too late for a school to hire for September anyway. I was almost home and I dreaded having to wait for a call with all these thoughts in my head. Just five minutes before I reached home, my phone rang and I couldn't help but answer while driving (my car didn't have a hands-free system installed). On the other end of the line was the Headmaster, who asked me if this was a good time to talk. Of course, I said yes and pulled into the fuel station. I stopped and switched off the engine so that I could hear properly. But I could not believe what I heard; I couldn't believe that I actually made it this time. I was offered the job as a teacher of French, they wanted me, I did it. It was an overwhelming feeling to finally have been accepted. The Headmaster explained that the school and my Head of Department would be in touch with me over the next few weeks to go through my on-boarding, but I was too exhilarated to produce a good response. All I could say was "thank you so much, I'm so happy, I don't know what to say", rush the last few metres back home and tell my family "I got the job, I'm starting in September".

5. Here comes the Newly Qualified Teacher

My classroom, my rules…?

So, there I was, some traumatic months and a rejuvenating summer later, in my own classroom. My first task as an officially qualified teacher was to decorate the walls with useful displays. The time had come to put up those grammar and vocabulary posters that I had always found ridiculous as I thought: "How are the children supposed to learn all these things, if they are right in front of them, ready to use and copy from?" Despite these thoughts, I did as I was asked to and covered my classroom walls with some French grammar and vocabulary. I was too overwhelmed and excited about the fact that I was going to be on my own in the room without another teacher, who always seems to know it better. However, I also realised that by being alone I was responsible for everything that happens in the classroom, which made me a little nervous. I went through phases of my brain telling me “Yes, you can do this! Finally, you’re by yourself and you own this room! You’re going to smash this!” or “Are you able to do this? You will have to handle every problem by yourself! What if the kids are horrible?” It was a back and forth in my head but I was told that these feelings were just normal and that I would be fine. My colleague, who was going to be my mentor during this first year of teaching, also called NQT (Newly Qualified Teacher) year, calmed me down and encouraged me to think positively. She, my other colleagues in the languages department, and my head of department assured me that whatever happened, I was not alone and that I could always count on their help. With their words in mind, I started welcoming my first classes into my room.

The first couple of days went quite smoothly and I was happy with myself. I mainly had to teach Year 7s and Year 8s, who were very keen and relatively easy to engage and manage. Especially the little ones were quite impressionable. As they were as new as I was at that school, I could make any impression I wanted on them. So, I went with being the tough B… It was when I encountered my first Year 9 class when all my confidence went down the drain. The second the class entered my room they were loud and impudent. They were barely interested in what I had to say. I was not able to finish a sentence without being interrupted at least once. Very quickly I spotted the trouble makers in that class and I sensed that I would be in difficult situations with them. After this class, I already dreaded my other Year 9 groups. I remember how I just wanted to disappear into the ground after this one hour of battling against the noise of 14-year-olds and not teaching them any French. I kept beating myself up over this lesson and was endlessly disappointed. The first two weeks were an eye-opener. I hadn't realised until a couple of weeks into the term what kind of students I would have to deal with. Apparently, the children attending that school had in general a reputation of being rude and some of them nasty. I encountered the latter type very early in my career as a newly qualified teacher. Already in my approximately third week of teaching, I had to face a Year 9 girl, whom I will call Amber, swearing at me. It was the second lesson I had with the class she was in and she was talking to her neighbour continuously and making irrelevant and rude comments for the entire first half of the lesson. When I calmly tried to discipline her, she back-chatted or completely ignored me as if I wasn't even there. So, I decided to remove her from my classroom and send her to a colleague of mine where she spent the rest of the lesson. Although Amber was supposed to come and see me afterwards so that I could do some restorative justice, she did not return so that I had to chase her in one of my free periods. I looked up her timetable and the room she was in and found her. She was already unhappy about the fact that I had come to disturb her in another lesson so that she did not want to talk to me at all. I explained to her that I just wanted a clean slate and that we could have a fresh start next lesson, but she did not seem to be interested. She kept claiming that I sent her away for no reason. While she was talking, a lot was going on in my head. Things like "Are you seriously denying that you were chatting throughout the whole lesson?!", "How dare you talk to me in that tone?!" or "Don't look at me as if I was a piece of sh...!" It was a terrible feeling being talked to like this while I just meant well and wanted to have peace. And when I thought it could not get worse, it did. Since the girl would not listen and drop her attitude I "threatened" her with having to contact her parents about this and that she still has to attend a detention with me. This kicked her off and she shouted "Oh you f***ing bi***!" and went back into the classroom, leaving me, unable to believe what I had just been called by a child who was nearly half my age and the jaws of other students in the corridor dropped. I had to escalate this to someone. I could not let her get away with such rudeness and disrespect! Frankly, I took this quite personally and at that time it was the most horrible experience for me. My mentor assured me that Amber didn't only behave like this with me and that she had problems with almost every teacher. According to my mentor, Amber was an intimidating girl who had no respect whatsoever for the adults around her. Still, at the end of that day, I went home wondering how a child could talk to me like that. Who knew it could get worse...? So, the incident was escalated to the department's line manager, who decided that the girl be removed from my lessons for a few weeks so that she could calm down and have a fresh start. That way, I did not have to deal with her, but somehow the class was still unpleasant and other students started to play up. You would think that the issue with that girl would have been solved, but what happened next took it to another level. She purposefully and continuously interrupted my lessons with other classes and one day, after school, when I was alone in my room and doing some marking she knocked on my window and shouted "I don't like you, you're a bad teacher!" She just would not leave me alone and kept holding a grudge for having her removed from my class, according to her, unreasonably. Since this was now regarded as a bullying case, she was told to stay away from me completely and if she did otherwise, she would get into big trouble. Honestly speaking, being treated that way by a teenager had a huge impact on me. It damaged my ego and my confidence significantly. It made me feel horrible about myself, although I knew that it wasn't my fault. My thoughts were fuelled even more when lessons with a so-called Set 1 Year 9 class went down the drain each time I saw them. To quickly explain what "set" means, in most schools in England, students are divided into different groups. In some, the sets don't make a difference as all groups are so-called mixed-ability. However, the experience I had was that the students were put into different sets according to their ability. This means that in set 1 you would find the kids who supposedly are bright and strong in that subject and the higher the set, the weaker the students become. In some schools though, certain subjects are somehow linked so that a student might be really good at German, but didn't do well in Technology and French so that he had to stay in a lower set, for instance set 3 or 4, maybe even set 5. I asked my Head of Department for support as Set 1 classes are a pressure point. They are expected to continue with French at GCSE level and therefore to do well in lessons and their assessments. However, these students' conduct was beyond abnormal for a class that was supposed to be bright and ambitious. Like the other Year 9 class, these children wouldn't stop chatting and disrupting lessons. The only difference was that these kids were arrogant and thought they knew everything better than their teacher. I dreaded each and every lesson with them until my Head of Department stepped in and had a good "shout" at them. After that it went much better, they were more settled and seemed to be more focused and realised that I could actually teach them something. With the class being more approachable, I also started to soften and developed a nice relationship with some of the kids; until the new girl (I am going to call her Clara) came.

The new girl

She had moved to outer London from the countryside. Apparently, Clara was very intelligent or rather, as they say, gifted and talented. Though to me, she didn't make a good impression. She brought an imbalance into the class that I worked so hard with on a healthy relationship. She stirred up the chatty girls and didn't produce work of a "gifted and talented" standard, but rather did the bare minimum. When I caught her being disruptive, she acted as if she never opened her mouth and pretended to take notes or copy from the board. I was boiling inside; I hated the way she behaved and how she unsettled my class. The most annoying thing was that she actually knew answers to my questions and understood the lessons. Why is this annoying? Because there is nothing more frustrating than a kid that is supposedly extremely intelligent but wants to be cool at the same time and therefore spoils your lessons.

As I was struggling my way through the first term, Christmas approached and brought about some warmth into the school. Little festive events lightened the gloomy winter mood, lessons were less tense as all teachers were doing Christmas activities and the students were going around distributing season's greetings and little presents to their teachers. If I had been insecure and disheartened over the past few weeks, those friendly gestures from some of my students certainly brightened my days and I felt so much better about everything; that means the place I was in, the children, the teaching, and myself. The highlight of the term was a Christmas slash thank you card from a student whom I had given the chance to move up a set. She was so grateful that she wrote me a card although I wasn't teaching her anymore. It was the best feeling ever. It made all the struggle and negative experiences worthwhile. So, with all the festive spirit in the air, I finished my very first term rather smoothly and on good terms. I cannot describe how much I was looking forward to two weeks of complete relaxation, unlike during the half-term holiday where I was preparing lessons and marking assessments. Christmas was going to be free of work and I knew I deserved it.

Fun fact: as I realised over the years, every teacher on the first day or second after a holiday longer than a week will feel like that holiday never happened. The minute you are back in school, in your classroom, surrounded by children, dealing with rudeness and poor behaviour or working hard to challenge the more able or dedicated ones, you feel like you have never had the two-week Christmas holiday. The same applies to the six-week summer holiday! Every teacher on the second day of term: "Summer holiday? I don't remember having one!" or "I need a holiday from the holidays" or "I'm ready for another holiday". And I was feeling just the same. Especially when I found out that the mother of that oh so clever girl Clara in my Year 9 set 1 class demanded that the teachers of her precious daughter differentiate the work for her because she was so bright. We had to give her more challenging tasks and more work to do, which meant for me as a new teacher: more work, more planning, more worries. What a great start to the new term. With the help of my colleagues, I was able to provide that girl, whose name I probably will never forget (you will find out soon why) with extra material for her to work through. I was told not to let her loose, to make her work as much as possible, even if it means that she cannot participate in the lesson. For her, the lesson was supposed to be a little extra on the side while she was working through some GCSE level worksheets. Should I feel bad saying that I felt a sense of pleasure when Clara raised her hand to ask for help or to say that she couldn't do it? In my head I would go like "Aaaawww, you don't know this? Seems like you're not THAT smart after all..." but of course I would go over to her (I sat her at the back corner of the classroom, away from everyone else) and support her. The other kids took the Mickey out of her for completing different work than them and this clearly irritated her. I didn't have much pity though, as it infuriated me so much that this girl was so full of herself, thinking she is the smartest and coolest person ever. I know it sounds childish and stupid to be thinking this way of a teenager who was only half my age, but I couldn't help it. I'm just human after all. Nevertheless, I did my duty and made the other kids stop interfering with Clara's "treatment". I also tried to put her in a positive light by saying that she was more advanced and therefore was completing more challenging work and that if someone needed help, they could ask her.

So, for a few weeks, I was focused on keeping that girl occupied in my lessons and her mother happy. I thought I had been doing a good job, since I didn't hear anything further about having to differentiate even more. I was pretty happy with how things went. Especially my other classes finally settled well, as if someone had applied a switch on almost all the students during the Christmas holidays. I was told that the hardest bit is the first term as the students get to know their teacher and push their boundaries. Once they see you coming back even after everything they "have done to you", they calm down, at least most of them. The fact that the children were more tranquil made me be more at peace and actually enjoy my lessons. This state of calm and pleasure didn't last very long. I was becoming slightly nervous and agitated when the Year 9 parents' evening approached. I had delivered good performances during previous evenings for Year 8 and Year 10, but somehow this one made me more anxious than the other ones. I blamed this anxiety on the fact that I was already struggling with that year group and that the mother of my most favourite and supposedly brightest student had made an appointment with me. Not just any appointment, but the very first one available. I was stressed about it, rightly so.

Parents' Evening Trauma

Although I was not looking forward to this appointment at all and on the inside was battling against my anxiety, I welcomed mother and child warmly. I won't forget the smirk on that girl's face. It was as if she knew what was coming, and probably she did. Once they had sat down, I started my little speech about how capable and skilled Clara was and how well she was getting on with her GCSE worksheets. I was told to sweet-talk the mother with the positives and not to aggravate her with the rather irritating behaviour and attitude of her daughter, or to put it differently, the truth. I wasn't entirely lying about Clara. She was bright and capable after all; it was just the way she conducted herself in my classroom that annoyed me to the core. But I left those details out of my description of her. However, no matter how nicely I portrayed her daughter in my report, the mother didn't seem to be interested in it at all, because she seemed to have come with a mission; the mission to knock me to the ground. I had barely finished my part when she began her attack. I don't even know where to begin to describe the emotions that I was going through when this woman accused me of being unable to teach her daughter French. Her grades in French had dropped since she moved schools and came to my class, where she was bored and didn't learn anything. I couldn't believe what I heard. What I could believe less was the fact that Clara was sitting right next to her mother, listening to her how she gave me a hard time and thereby completely undermined my authority. The worst part is that I was not given one second to express my opinions about her accusations. Not that I would have been capable of professionally coming up with some good counter arguments, but the mother just wouldn't stop telling me how bad a teacher I was. I was able to get my Head of Department, who sat right next to me, to assist me with this appointment. When she was part of the conversation, the mother started to refer to me in 3rd person. I had to listen to phrases such as "no offence against this young lady here, but she clearly doesn't have the experience to teach my daughter French" or "Clara doesn't learn anything valuable in her lessons". Although my Head of Department contested this by pointing out that I have been providing Clara with extra material of GCSE level, mum was not happy because Clara could sit and do worksheets at home, she doesn't need to go to school for that. There was no winning with this woman, and so even my Head of Department had to give in by saying that we will work out how to move forward. On this note, mother and daughter (still smirking away) finally stood up and moved on to destroy the next teacher's soul. This is how I felt anyway. As if someone has torn everything I had worked for my whole life into pieces. I was sent to the staff room to take a break after this demoralising first appointment. I didn't have to be told twice. As I left the main hall to walk up to the staff room, all the tears that I'd been holding back since that woman opened her mouth, or actually since I started my job at that school, started to well up and blur my vision. I wasn't yet ready to cry. I still had the whole evening to survive and other parents to meet. So, I pulled myself and every little drop of motivation together and went back to the hall, not at all ready to meet more parents. The rest of the evening went by in a blur. I had nothing but this horrible first appointment in my mind and it didn't really help, although she meant well, that my Head of Department said that in her 13 years of teaching, she has never met such a parent and never had such an appointment. Of course, she wanted to make me feel better but it made me start to think that maybe I actually was the problem. Maybe I was incapable of teaching those children, perhaps I was not good enough. With these thoughts in the back of my head, making me all stiff and nervous, and the fear that I would have another soul crushing meeting, I somehow managed to remain calm and professional on the outside. Each time I welcomed another parent to my desk, I dreaded what they were going to say and that I'd start crying then and there, making a complete fool of myself. Thankfully, the rest of the evening remained eventless. I was not in the position to take more than what I was already dealing with. When I finally sat in the car to go home around eight o'clock in the evening, I melted down. First, I called my parents to let them know that I was only leaving school then and would talk to them the next day. My voice gave away that I was not in a good place, so I poured my heart out. And I did it again when I reached home and my husband asked me what was wrong because my long face revealed it. He was so used to guessing my mood when I came home from school as it had been the same for the last year and a half. My visage was either neutral, which meant that I had an okay day, or troubled which signalled that something had happened and I was distressed. Only very rarely would I return with a happy face. Anyhow, to me this whole parents' evening incident was such a devastating experience. Nothing that anyone said made me actually feel better. I guess everyone deals with such things differently. Some don't get affected at all, others take it to heart and make a big deal out of it. Obviously, I belonged (and still do) to the latter group. I was told that I feel this way because I am taking my job seriously and because I am so dedicated that I take such comments personally. Which is probably true, but what upset me probably the most was the fact that this mother was being harsh and disrespectful to me with her daughter sitting right next to her and probably having the time of her life, because her mother ripped a teacher apart in her presence. How was I going to pull through the rest of the year having to teach that class and having to see that girl? What was she going to tell her friends? Are any of those students going to respect me at all? So many questions that I didn't know how to answer and maybe didn't want to know the answer to. I was completely discombobulated. I was going through hell when I got out of bed and made my way to school the next morning. It just didn't feel right. Why would someone go back to the place where they have been robbed of their dignity? Pretending to be strong was my strategy but it didn't really work out. After two lessons, I had another melt-down. My Head of Department arranged someone to cover my next lesson and sat down with me to talk. She had also informed the Headmaster, which was so embarrassing, but luckily, he was on my side that time and assured me that he knew that I was a dedicated and a good teacher. Apparently, that mother was giving grief to other teachers as well, but as we've established, everyone deals with situations differently. Both decided that I couldn't teach being so distraught and insisted I went home early to recover from all this over the weekend. I had a quick word with my mentor since we didn't get the chance to speak after parents evening. She had always been so kind and encouraging towards me and was really emphatic regarding this whole Clara matter. She agreed that I should go home and get some distance from school. So, I packed my bag and drove into an early weekend, with a damp feeling of not wanting to return on Monday. On the flipside, it would be the last week before half-term, where I was going to see my family in Germany and forget all about school. With this in mind, I scraped together my last bits of energy and drove to work on Monday. It was really calming and reassuring how everyone was looking after me and checking on me. It made being there much easier. And it was getting even better. Towards the end of the week, right on time for half-term, I was called into the Headmaster's office. I went in, thinking it would have to do with that parents evening a week ago, but to my surprise and pleasure, I was offered a permanent contract after the NQT year. I was over the moon, it felt like all my hard work and suffering was worth it. And finally, I found closure for last week, too. Now, nothing mattered to me. I just had to go through another interview as a formality and sign the contract. Whatever any parent would have to say about me in the future, I was sure that I was able to stand above it because my colleagues and the Headmaster appreciated my hard work. It seemed like everyone in the department already knew before me because when I came back to the languages building to tell everyone, they already congratulated me. I couldn't wait to get home to tell my husband the good news, so I called him to share my joy with him right away and we already made plans for our future. With this great news, I finished off the rest of the week with a positive vibe and went into the half-term holidays more confident than ever before. It was a great experience being able to celebrate my achievement with a short trip to my hometown in Germany. However, this half-term holiday took an unexpected turn.

6. Please take the next exit

Good news(?)

Back home, we found out that I was pregnant, which was a pleasant surprise. But obviously, things would change and I started to become anxious about my situation at work. In addition to that I was suffering from morning sickness or rather all-day sickness and couldn't make it to school for more than two or three days a week since school started after half-term. This again stressed me out because I was worried about what they might think of me calling in sick two or three days a week, so my husband and I decided that we should tell my Head of Department about my pregnancy. Once I had shared my news with her, I felt much more at ease thinking that now that someone knows why I am not coming into school for complete weeks, it wouldn't affect my NQT status or even worse, I wouldn't be made redundant. I asked my Head of Department not to share my news with anyone for now as I wanted to pass the three-months-mark before officially telling anyone, whether at work or in my private life. She assured me that my secret was safe with her and I felt relaxed immediately. For the next two weeks, I stayed at home if I couldn't make it out of bed due to sickness and nausea without having a bad conscience. What happened next seems to have got the ball rolling and a train of mishaps started to develop right in front of me. One morning, when I had just arrived at school, my Head of Department called me into her office. She wanted to discuss the current situation, meaning my pregnancy and the fact that I had asked her to keep it quiet until I was ready to share the news. She began asking when I was thinking of telling the department and the Headmaster. When I said that I wasn't planning on telling anyone very soon, I could tell by her facial expression that I will not be able to stick to this plan. She said that she understands me and my situation, however, she is being put into a difficult position where she is having to lie to colleagues about my whereabouts and the reason why I'm not in school half the time. Immediately, I felt a sense of guilt building up inside of me and without even thinking, I offered to tell the Headmaster about my pregnancy straight away. My Head of Department seemed relieved and grateful for my decision and said that he should be free right now and that he would be happy to speak to me in his office. So, I made my way to the main building and requested to speak with the Headmaster, who, as predicted, was welcoming me into his office without hesitation. When I broke the news to him, he was very positive about it. He congratulated me and then raised the topic of maternity and cover. As he was talking, he accompanied me to the HR Manager's office to discuss the further plan, which was to still have an interview for the sake of formality, sign the contract after Easter and then settle everything regarding maternity cover. I couldn't believe that everything was going so well and so positively. I left the office, feeling secure and vibrant thinking that I would be sorted for the next few years since I had scored a permanent work contract and a convenient outcome for my pregnancy on top of that. At that point, I didn't know that I was going to be disappointed to the same extent that I was happy. For now, I was over the moon and so relieved. This happiness didn't last long as every single day started to be a struggle. I was already stressed and struggling with my sickness, but the children's behaviour was becoming more and more unbearable.

Attack

It came to a point that just going to work made me feel sick. Especially after the incident with my USB stick, I was shocked by how vicious, yet creative these children could be. A year 7 boy, who was not doing very well in my subject and who was already on my radar for his challenging behaviour was plotting against me and I had no idea. I had to remove him from my lesson a couple of times due to his chattiness and contact his parents about his distracting activities during class. Of course, it was never his fault and he always had something to say in his defence. However, what he did in the end was beyond my capability to accept and understand that this action came from an eleven-year-old. One day, when I came into my classroom in the morning, my computer set-up was completely messed up. No wire and cable were where it was supposed to be. I had to use my time that I had planned for some morning lesson preparation to put back together my computer, which already stressed me out. My first two lessons went quite smoothly despite the little hiccup in the morning. I went on break duty, enjoyed my apple and was happy when the bell rang so that I could go inside and just get over with the next lesson with the "lovely" Year 9. I had a surprisingly good lesson with them and for me that was the day done as Year 9 was always the worst lesson for me. The next lesson would just be with Year 7 and my only "problem" would be that boy. At least, this is what I thought. A few minutes into the lesson, my PowerPoint presentation, my screen, and my computer were doing their own thing. When I clicked forward, it went back a slide, when I opened a new folder, it closed again and all these weird things. I had absolutely no clue what was happening but because it was just Year 7, I sort of managed to keep them calm. Of course, they were laughing and starting to play up. A little threat of a phone call home, a detention and some extra homework did its job. I improvised with some text book work wondering what had happened to my computer that was absolutely fine just before break. The lesson ended positively given the fact that I had no control over my computer and my stress level was just constantly high due to my pregnancy. I dismissed the kids and it was only then, just before going into lunch, that I noticed my missing USB stick. It was not just any USB stick, but the one with everything on it. All my resources that I have ever made, all my lessons that I had planned, all my NQT stuff was there. Basically, hundreds of hours of work were saved on that USB stick and it was gone. I spent my entire lunch time searching for it because I became paranoid that I had misplaced it somewhere, although I knew that I had put it into my computer in the morning, since I had taught all my lessons from it that day. When I realised that the stick was nowhere to be found and the lunch break was coming to an end, I shared this with my colleagues and my Head of Department because I was completely lost and not experienced enough to just wing a lesson on my own. My colleagues reassured me that the USB stick must be somewhere and they would help me after school to find it. My mentor sent me a lesson to use for last period. Of course, in that moment, for the next hour, that had saved my life. However, the thought of my USB stick being lost for good made me want to throw up. I somehow managed to pull through the last lesson of the day, another Year 7 lesson, but all I could think about was my USB stick that literally meant everything to me at that time. I must have shown that I was tense and stressed out as a couple of students asked me if everything was okay and I shared my worry with them. Amongst all the tension, this was probably one of the sweetest moments that I experienced during my time at that school, because the students felt for me and tried to make me feel better. They offered to help me look for the pen drive and tried to cheer me up. We talked through what happened since after break and only then I realised that something must have happened between the end of period two and period 4, because my computer was working just fine in this last lesson. On top of that, one of the students sitting at the back found a suspicious note on the floor that said "Dont look at me or she well now that somethings up". Yes, you're reading correctly, this is how it was written, with spelling and grammar mistakes. And I recognised this handwriting just too well! It was the handwriting of that troublesome Year 7 boy and the note was lying right next to where he sat. After I had dismissed my last class of that day, I took the note to my Head of Department and presented to her my evidence for my suspicion that this boy had to have something to do with all the happenings in my classroom today and my lost USB stick. She took the note and promised me that she would investigate it first thing next morning and comforted me, knowing my little secret. After this nerve-wracking day, I felt like opening up to my mentor and just telling her that I was pregnant. It all became too much and I felt like I had to release myself from the burden of having to hide the fact that I was pregnant. So, I went to her classroom and was trying to make conversation as I was struggling for words to make my announcement. The reason for my nervousness was the fact that my mentor, just like me but on a larger scale, had gone through a traumatic experience in the past year and I was worried that my news would change our relationship. Despite these thoughts, I managed to finally spit it out and to my pleasure, her reaction was one that I had not expected at all. She said: "Me, too!" For me, this could not have gone in any better way! I was so happy for her and for myself and I was so excited that I had someone who was going through this beautiful yet daunting experience with me. She was happy for me, too and we exchanged more information about our pregnancies and how it was going for us.

During the conversation, it turned out that we were just a couple of weeks apart. As I was chatting about the pregnancy with my mentor, I had forgotten about my horrible day for a few minutes, but when I got ready to go home, I remembered. It struck me that somehow, I had to manage the next few days without my resources or that I had to plan numerous lessons all over again from scratch within a couple of days. Only the thought of that made my stomach churn. I went home, already having decided that I was going to ditch work the next day. At home, I reported all the happenings to my husband in tears and that I'd just wanted to quit, that I didn't want to go to school anymore and that it was all too much for me to handle. As usual, he comforted me, gave me a pep-talk and I was back on track. At that time, I blamed the pregnancy hormones and the stress of having to somehow manage through the day being constantly nauseous for my thoughts of quitting teaching. I kept thinking that everything would be better once I had finished my NQT year and once I had delivered my baby. It was a roller-coaster ride of emotions, but every time I managed to pull myself up after an emotional melt-down.

I stayed off work the following day as planned saying that I was really sick from all the stress and tension the day before. I probably would have survived somehow, but I could just not face having another difficult day at school, especially looking at my full timetable for that day. At the same time, it seemed too much of an effort to me. My mentor was extremely supportive in this matter and advised me to prioritise my well-being over work and to take care of myself. I knew she was right, yet I felt bad and guilty when I was in bed instead of in my classroom. The good thing was that I turned into an expert for making cover work sheets out of PowerPoint presentations. I spent the day pondering what could have happened to my USB stick, how I was going to manage without all my resources and that it was just stupid of me to have everything on just that one pen drive instead of securing my material on either my personal laptop or the school shared drive. Had I done any of that, I would not have been in the situation that I was in. As I was thinking about what could have been and could be, my mentor texted me that she was back home from school and that she could now drop off the sets of student books I had asked her to bring home. We used to live in the same town, so we would do each other little favours like that, now and then. When we saw each other, she gave me some interesting updates on my lost USB stick. My Head of Department had done her investigation and found out that behind everything that had happened the previous day was a master plan of that little Year 7 fellow. Not only did he have a device to control my computer and a spare remote to take over the projector, he was also the one who had unplugged all wires on my computer in the morning. But here comes the disaster beyond all expectations: he stole my USB stick, took it home, transferred everything onto his computer and erased all contents from my device. I could say or do nothing but stand there with an open mouth and disbelief in my eyes. Such a plot against me from an eleven-year-old, just because he hated French and I had contacted his parents about his behaviour?! Yes, I had to discipline him a few times because of his inappropriate conduct, but not in my worst night-mare would I have imagined that a child of this young age would plan a proper revenge plot of this scale. I took the books from my mentor, who assured me not to worry and that our Head of Department as well as SLT (senior leadership team) were on the little brat's case. I was in pure shock. And my trauma just got worse. The whole thing became a police case since what he had done was considered theft and breach of privacy. The police searched his bedroom and his computer for more school-related sensitive information, but the father was useless as his only comment to this was that his son must have had a reason for doing something like this! Can you imagine that after all that this child had done, his father was blaming me for his actions?! On top of that, I had to have a meeting with that boy and the designated safeguarding and behaviour representative of my school. I didn't even want to see that face anymore, the face that had caused me so much mental and physical stress and pain. And this child even had the guts to say that, when he was asked why he thought he could do such things, he did it because he hates French and that he didn't like me. I sat there, flabbergasted at this response, feeling numb, infuriated, threatened, appalled, scandalised and sad, all at the same time, trying to keep my composure because I was a professional and could not let myself down to his level, trying not to shout at him "And I hate you!". I was absolutely horrified.

He was made to apologise to me, but his apology was not at all sincere and I was not in the position to accept it and that's what I said in a way as professional as I managed at that point in time. I was dismissed from the meeting because I had to teach in a few minutes. When I left that office, all I could do was cry. In what place was I, where children go as far as causing a teacher, an adult, a professional, this much distress and suffering? The verdict for him was to not come to my lessons anymore until further notice and so now two students were banned from my class. What a great thing to say. He returned my USB stick with all my resources (he was made to drag them back onto the pen drive from his computer), but somehow it didn't trigger the reaction I had hoped for within myself. The more dominant thoughts in my mind were now: "Do I really want to be here? Do I really want to deal with these kinds of things for the rest of my life?"

Endurance

This incident set the tone for the rest of the term. My Year 9 classes were a pain as usual and there was no light in sight at the end of the tunnel. In fact, more students decided to give their teachers a hard time. I had to deal with at least one troublemaker in almost every class, even in Year 7. Constantly, I spent my time after school supervising my detainees or writing complaint emails to parents, in which I tried to describe their child's poor behaviour to them without being condescending, personal or unprofessional. I felt like I was not teaching the kids my subject, but how to behave and to respect adults and teachers. In fact, I did not feel like a teacher but like a childminder or social worker. All my preparation and planning would seem a waste of time as, day in day out, I was spending more time managing the behaviour of the children than doing my actual job. The fact that with every single time I opened my mouth, I felt like vomiting due to my pregnancy sickness just made everything even more irritating and difficult. As the term progressed, some students settled and gave up on pushing their boundaries, however some just discovered that they could do that. Especially, Y8 students turned, slowly but surely, into the hormone-loaded teenagers that they would be after the summer holidays, Y9s. I had difficulties especially with one girl in a Y8 class, who I am going to call Millie and who was never very noticeable, but all of a sudden decided to give me a hard time. It became her normal routine to be in my detention after school on the days she had French with me. Then, this as well escalated as she stopped attending those. When I emailed her mother, all I got was empty promises that she would make sure that her daughter would not behave this way anymore. In class, when I confronted Millie about her poor behaviour and attitude and tried to intimidate her by saying I would have to contact her mother again, she just back-chatted saying that her mother does not care about French and actually never told her off because of my emails. I could not believe this until Y8 parents evening, when Millie and her mother sat right there in front of me and completely ignored me waving at them. They had not made an appointment, which I was already surprised about as I had asked to see them, but the fact that I had to stand up, walk towards them and invite them over to my desk, although they saw me waving, threw me off. Was this something to laugh or be wound up about? I did not know anymore. During our conversation, it was very clear that Millie's mother, indeed, did not seem to care about her daughter's attitude and behaviour in my lessons at all. Although she kept saying to her daughter how disrespectfully she was behaving, I could feel that none of this was genuine. I just thought to myself "I'm doing my job, I'm trying and if it doesn't work, then there is not much I can do!" After this parents' evening, I dreaded the lessons with her even more, because now I knew that I did not have any support from home. The worst thing was, this girl had the ability to draw the whole class, apart from a handful of quiet students, into her mess. She behaved in a way that nobody could concentrate and almost every other student in that class followed her lead. I could not get rid of her either, because she just would not leave and when she left, she would just take another girl with her, who also would just happily follow her. It was a nightmare in the daytime and to add to that, there were other kids in the same class, who were difficult to deal with right from the start. I was literally battling my way through every single lesson with that class and at the end of it I would be so exhausted, as if I had taught five lessons in a row. I would go home crying almost every day and slowly, I realised that I didn't want to feel this way for the rest of my life. Although my colleagues reassured me saying that it will all become better and easier with time, I could not imagine this to be true. With each day, my mind adjusted itself a little more to the idea of quitting; quitting the NQT year and quitting teaching. The only thing that kept me from making a firm decision was, on the one hand, the fact that I was offered a permanent contract, which made me think that I must be doing *something* right and that I must be good at what I was doing. On the other hand, my family kept encouraging me, repeating the words of my colleagues as if they had heard them speak. I felt like I had hardly any say in this. Each argument I brought up supporting my idea of following another career path, was finally downplayed by the rhetorical question from my parents or my husband: "Is this why you have studied and worked so hard over the last six or seven years?" And that shut my mouth and my mind, because deep down, I didn't want to just quit like that, having strived to become a teacher for so long. However, looking back, I knew myself too well and should have listened to my instincts back then. The fact that I had never felt about something this intensely in a bad way had to mean something. I knew that it wasn't just a phase or a whim. Yet, I listened to my family and tried to make myself believe that I would be fine. I continued, for my family, in the hope that, like everyone said, all would be easier once this year was over.

As if all this, the battle with Millie and the struggle with my thoughts, was not enough to deal with, I had to face further annoyances from another Y7 boy, whose fictional name will be Tim. Just like Millie, Tim decided to be annoying out of the blue and the parents had no other excuse than blaming me for their son's actions. No matter what I did to encourage the boy or to find little good things that he did, he'd always find a way to spoil my lesson or to revert back to misbehaviour. I would then have to report his misconduct to the parents, who then would defend him and so on. It was a vicious cycle that was just draining and frustrating. I then decided to completely ignore him, which seemed to work, but of course as soon as I had him "under control", other children started to play up and that class quickly became, not only my, but everyone's least favourite Y7 class. At least, I was not the only teacher who found them annoying. The whole staff was dreading class 7W and that made me feel a lot better. The days went by and I somehow survived each and every day without throwing up during working hours. The Easter holidays that I was longing for so badly finally arrived and I was looking forward to just being able to stay at home and relax for two weeks. Well, as much as a teacher can relax over any holidays as I still had to do some work in preparation for the next term, but at least I didn't have to travel to school and face all the stress of having to manage those children's behaviour! Plus, I was going to complete the formalities of my permanent contract after the Easter holidays. At least that's what I thought.

Bombshell

Back at school, after the holidays, I was eagerly awaiting an email from the Headmaster with an invitation for an informal interview and to sign the contract afterwards. When in the second week of term, I still hadn't received such an email, I took the initiative to send one myself asking what I had to do for the upcoming interview. I had a reply from the Head teacher's assistant just a few minutes later. In the message it said I should come to his office during break time. And so, I did, filled with excitement and expecting nothing but the completion or discussion of the formalities of my permanent contract and my maternity leave. These expectations were stamped out quickly when the Head teacher started with "I'm afraid, I have some bad news" after he had invited me to have a seat. He carried on claiming that the number of students who opted for GCSE French next year was smaller than expected and that therefore they wouldn't be able to keep their promise. At that moment, I wasn't quite sure what he was trying to say. Afraid of being right, I asked for clarification by asking if it means that my contract ends in August. The answer left me devastated and I could feel something crumble inside of me. After I had asked my question, he confirmed: "I'm afraid, yes. We won't be able to afford another full-time member of staff with such a small number of GCSE students and fewer teaching hours. I am very sorry." And all I could bring out of my mouth was: "That's understandable, it's okay. Thanks for letting me know." The Head teacher saw me out of his office and, not having fully comprehended what I just heard, I went up to the staff room, where I found my mentor and another good colleague having their snacks. When I told them about what had just happened, they were outraged and in disbelief. They tried to comfort me and told me how well I was taking the situation, but what they didn't know was how shattered I was inside. Both of them couldn't believe that the number of GCSE students would make such an impact and on top of that, that I was told such distressing news between lessons during a short break, without consideration for the fact that I was a pregnant woman.

For me, one of the major factors to continue teaching was now eliminated. There would be no permanent position. After having my baby, I would have to apply for another position again at God knows how many schools before I could secure a post. And the worst though of all: if I found a school, I would have to establish myself all over again. I was 80% sure that I did not want to do this. The other 20% were still thoughts like "Why quit when being a teacher is all I ever wanted?" and "I would disappoint my family if I quit".

So, with my heart and thoughts anywhere else but in the classroom, I finished teaching my classes for the day and went straight home, without staying a minute longer. Because why should I? All the stress and all the work for a majority of children who did not appreciate any of my efforts and for a position that had an expiry date anyway. Of course, I started out knowing that my contract was a fixed term one, but you know what it feels like when you're given something and then have it taken away again. I felt treated unfairly and I was disappointed in my Head of Department. I now began to think that she might have cornered me into telling the Headmaster about my pregnancy early enough for selfish reasons. I wondered if she wanted to sort out the department for the coming year and not have to do this in the summer term, at the completion of my 20 weeks of pregnancy, when I actually could have revealed it. I didn't understand the world anymore, I felt so betrayed and overwhelmed, I just wanted to leave that place. You might think that I am being over-sensitive and taking everything too personally and I admire people who can just brush every rudeness and maltreatment off and carry on as if nothing happened. For me, a nightmare had been unfolding in front of my very eyes since I had started out at this school.

That day, I just went home feeling numb and cried again at home, telling my husband about the news. We had planned everything out, counting on the maternity pay and my position for when I would go back after delivery. My husband claimed that they were getting rid of me so that they didn't have to hire a cover teacher and also pay for my maternity and that they had taken advantage of the fact that I hadn't signed an official contract, yet. For the first time, I saw this viewpoint, but I couldn't believe it. I didn't think that an educational institution would be so nasty and kept arguing against this idea of his. He insisted that he was right and we left it at that as there was no point in arguing over this. The fact was: I would have no job after August and we wouldn't be able to afford our flat and live on his salary alone. More and more anger rose inside of me when I realised how big the impact of this was. I calculated the months, weeks and days of how long I had to persevere at that place and started to countdown. The next morning, I called in sick, and cited feeling stressed and overwhelmed by this news as an excuse. And that's what I did more and more often for the remaining three months or so before the last day of term. If I didn't feel like getting up and going in, I'd call in sick and I was not bothered about what people, especially the leadership team, might think, because I was not going to be there next term anyway. If getting up and going into school was a struggle before, now it was torture. Of course, the students had no clue about my leaving at the end of term and I wanted to keep it that way. I could only imagine what they'd be like if they found out that I wasn't going to be here next term. On the bright side, the kinder children began to notice that I was pregnant and approached me with questions about whether I knew if it was a boy or a girl, what name the baby would have and if I could feel it move.

Nuisance after nuisance

These were the moments that kept me going for the last three months of the term and my time at that school. Short sequences of laughter and fun with particular children were very entertaining and I was very grateful for them. I stopped caring about what some kids had to say about my subject and my lessons and just accepted the fact that some kids just were horrible enough to spoil everything for the good ones. Not that my accepting this changed anything or made them behave any better, but it gave me some peace of mind. There was one thing however, that I had to pick up as it became personal. There was this girl, whom I will call Tania, in my Set 1, Year 9 class (of course), who had always been chatty and lively but generally worked hard and seemed like a nice kid. From one day to another, her behaviour changed and she began to copy some other girls' attitude which was detrimental to the lessons. She was talking and shouting out, making irrelevant comments throughout the lesson that distracted the others and was generally restless. It came to a point where I had to remove her from the lesson and take other measures, such as changing her seat, away from her friends, which she didn't like at all. In response, Tania then ganged up with her friends and shouted around my name in different variations whenever they were near or around me in the playground. I wouldn't mind students having nicknames for me, but this rather sounded like ridiculing rather than an act of fondness. I heard names such as "Ms Rag" or "Rags" or other versions followed by giggling and laughing. Maybe it was childish of me to take it to heart, but I just couldn't stand the fact that these children were making fun of my surname, as I found it extremely disrespectful. One day, I addressed this in class, insisting that if I ever made fun of any of their names, they and their parents would be straight on my case which could make me even lose my job. I thought that this would have made them understand and realise that making fun of anyone's name is just not right, but I could still hear them around school, carrying on with it. I saw no other choice but to finally contact Tania's mother as she seemed to be the trigger for it all. I explained in my email that her daughter had changed attitude and behaviour all of a sudden and that I had already taken all measures. The mother, in return, reacted in a way that I would never have expected. The email she wrote back sounded as if she was contesting and denying everything I had brought forward. She said that she hadn't brought her daughter up to be disrespectful and that she never had to read such an email from any teacher before. She wanted to have a meeting to discuss all this. And so, the meeting was arranged with myself, the language department's line manager, Tania and her mother. It was quite interesting and funny at the same time for me to see, how in this instance, the child was acting rather small and reserved in front of the parent, opposite to what I have seen previously and recently from her. My line manager and I had done some investigation and found out that Tania, not only became more prominent in my class, but also in other lessons where she was part of the main disruptors. This information seemed to come very shocking to the mother as no other teacher had contacted her, yet. It also turned around the whole direction of the situation, the mother not agreeing with my points, so that she now aimed her investigation and inquiry at her daughter who all of a sudden had little to say and just sat there with her arms crossed and staring at the floor. I put all cards on the table and also expressed how disappointed I was about her attitude, bearing in mind Tania's potential and she was made to apologise to me by her mother, who also gave me her full support to put in place any measures that I see fit for her daughter's behaviour in the future. The only thing Tania didn't admit was the name-calling, despite her mum asking her several times and obviously, in that case, there was nothing else myself or my line manager could do about it, but to just say that in general this is something inappropriate and shouldn't be done. The meeting ended with the mother wishing me all the best as she had noticed my bump and I went home feeling quite satisfied with the outcome. I had the feeling that Tania didn't expect at all that her mother would take the teachers' side and so she felt humiliated. For the rest of the year, Tania didn't talk to me during lessons, unless she couldn't read something on the board. She didn't participate or make any eye contact with me. And I was fine with it. I couldn't care less, to be honest. I felt like this with many things and funnily enough, it became slightly easier to go into school towards the end of the term as everything just left me indifferent since I wasn't going to be there in September anyway. I went through each lesson and through each "quarrel" without any engagement whatsoever and that took a whole load of stress off me. I began to think that maybe that this should have been the way to be right from the start: indifferent, untouched, and nonchalant. Did I make a mistake by caring too much? When I discussed this topic with my colleagues in my department, especially my mentor, reassured me that I had always been doing the right thing, right from the start. Teachers who were trying to befriend their students and who are liked by them are not automatically good teachers. In fact, apart from the good (and somewhat unhealthy) relationship they had with their students, everything else usually went rather badly for them. I didn't want to fully believe what I heard, until I myself heard some stories from children of what their other newly qualified teachers were doing during lessons so that they could catch up on their own work and time. From letting the students on their phone, to just putting on a movie, some people just did it and also reaped the compliments, from both students and other teachers, and the Headmaster. I found it extremely unfair that I was confronted with such a destiny while I was amongst the only two or three NQTs, who worked their socks off for the students' academic progress in our subjects and for the NQT programme (we had to gather everything we did to meet the national teacher standards in a huge file that then would be submitted for evaluation), yet I was the one who got "sacked" and those who barely did anything but be their students' friends were praised and promoted. What a charade this whole matter was in my eyes. I couldn't wait to finally get out of there.

About a month before the end of term, I was invited to an exit interview that was conducted by one of the school's governors. I didn't even know that such an interview existed and became a little nervous. I was sent a questionnaire that I was supposed to fill out with honest answers. The only thing was, I could not be honest. If I had been honest, I would have just been ranting and venting out all the frustration that accumulated over the past year and I am not the kind of person that just speaks their mind without thinking about the repercussions. One thing, however, I was honest about. During the Spring Term, a colleague of mine and I ran an Easter German club that took place in my classroom once a week at lunch time. I had created the resources and gave up my lunches during that time to provide some fun activities to children who were interested and came by. Our efforts and commitment were never praised or mentioned in any of the staff meetings, unlike similar projects of other subject departments. In fact, none of the language department's efforts stood out as much as the achievements of other subjects, not because the efforts and achievements were absent, but because little attention and importance was given to the subject by the leadership. This is not just my opinion, but had been voiced by my colleagues as well. So, in my exit interview, I mentioned how I was a little offended by the fact that my hard work and commitment towards the extra-curricular German club seemed to go unnoticed by the Headmaster and my Head of Department. This was the only completely honest comment I made, everything else was pretty much sweet-talk as I didn't want to get into trouble or create a big deal before I left. After the interview, I felt bad for even saying the thing about the Easter Club. I just hoped that nobody would take offence, but quickly remembered that even if they did, I didn't have to care about it since I had been treated badly and was going to leave.

The lasts

The last days approached fast. For the last couple of weeks, I was counting down to my "last lesson" with each class and got more and more excited that all this was coming to an end. But it also was in the last two weeks when students had finally found out that I was leaving and approached me. Quite a few expressed how sad they were and then there were others, who surprised me with comments such as "I didn't know you were leaving, Miss. I actually quite liked you" or "I know we didn't always agree in lessons but you're actually alright, Miss". And this came from Y9 students, one of whom really gave me a hard time sometimes! I didn't know how to feel; touched, emotional, happy, sad? It felt so strange. I wondered, why did they have to tell me now? What is the point in telling me this when I am leaving? But I suppose, (some) kids just don't think about their actions and how it might affect the other, especially when it is an adult and above all a teacher. It seems that all they care about is their own life, their friends and how someone makes them feel.

And so, the last day of term had arrived. Again, I can't quite express how I felt. Emotional on the one hand and relieved on the other. I actually only had two lessons to "teach" that day. I finished my time at that school with two free lessons and when the bell rang signalling the end of the day, I was able to identify how I felt. It was an overwhelming relief. If I had been alone a few more moments, I probably would have started to cry out loud, but my colleagues came to give me my leaving presents, which distracted me from my urge to weep and together, we went to the end of year teacher gathering outside behind the canteen. The staff had a little chit-chat amongst themselves, with drinks and snacks until the Headmaster started his speech. Staff and teachers who did something exceptional over the past academic year were praised and awarded with some nice little gifts, the NQTs were celebrated for finishing what was a tough year, and lastly, staff who were leaving were thanked and asked to say a few words. And this is the part when I became emotional and sad. My Head of Department presented a little speech that my department colleagues had prepared together which just made me cry. I declined the request to say a few words at first, because I was just sobbing, but then brought out a couple of sentences thanking everyone, especially my department for all the support throughout the year and the Headmaster for giving me the opportunity in the first place. Although I was quite disappointed and angry, I didn't have the heart to leave on bad terms. And this despite the fact that they actually went on and hired two part-time teachers after telling me that they did not have the funds to keep me as a full-time member of staff. I am not an expert on budgeting and human resources; however, I knew that this was how they avoided having to provide my maternity pay as well as hiring and paying a cover teacher. So, it seemed as if my husband was right after all and I had been tricked, but what could I do now? After the staff gathering, I went to my mentor's classroom to drop off my present for her unborn baby. We both seemed to feel a little awkward having to say good-bye, so I didn't stay long. I said a final word to everyone else in my department, grabbed the remaining bags with my belongings and made my way to the carpark. I can't quite pinpoint how I felt when leaving the school premises, but I remember that in my mind, I had already imagined this to be the last day in school for me. In any school. It was a little daunting as I was not sure how life would go on after I had my baby. What was I going to do, professionally? What other qualities and interests did I have? All I ever wanted and thought about was teaching languages and now I wanted to quit. So many thoughts of this sort were running through my mind. I managed to quieten the brain chatter by saying to myself: "First, you have to pop out this baby of yours." And so, I drove home, happy that I could finally just focus on myself and being pregnant.

7. Every mistake counts

I was enjoying the summer, especially now, that I didn't have to worry about next term and going back to school. It was a time of my life where I was the most relaxed, yet anxious at the same time. I would have lay-ins, go out with my husband whenever I fancied, or just stay at home, watch a movie and go to bed as early or as late as I wanted to. I knew that I had to make the most of this time before our off-spring would come into this world and occupy me for... well, forever. Sometimes, thoughts about my future career would pop in my head. Would I go back to teaching? If yes, will I be able to handle all the stress with a child of my own? If not, what would I be doing instead? I'd quickly brush them off, though and tell myself that I would be so busy and fulfilled once I had my baby that I won't have the time to think about work or will ever want to go back to work.

After giving birth, I was obviously overwhelmed with the new routines (or the fact that there was no routine?) and my new responsibilities as a mother. For a few months, I was indeed too occupied with my little one to realise that I actually missed going to work and leaving the house by myself, let alone having an income of my own. I missed being independent as well as free from commitments other than being a wife. Now, I was a mother and my job was to bring up my son, which struck me as not my only purpose in life. I realised that I could never be a stay-at-home mom. No matter how much I loved my baby and wanted to spend every minute with him, I also wanted to be my own person again and do something for myself. So, when my son was around seven months old, I started looking for jobs. I started off ignoring any teaching posts. I was looking for something that did not require any more time apart from the hours at the work place. My plan was to go to work, come home and spend the rest of the time with my family, not having to worry about the next day. During my job search, I had to face comments and listen to the advice from my husband, my in-laws and my parents. Why did I need to go to work now? Why can't I wait a few more months? If I had to work, I should look for a teaching job, because that's what I am trained to do. Everybody meant well, but to me it was just comprehendible why nobody understood my point of view. While I was giving my family's opinions some thought, I received a text message from my mentor, who told me about a vacancy at my old school. The one that had ditched me and where she was still working, but on maternity leave. Funnily enough, we delivered our babies on the same day and therefore shared another, more special, bond. The school were looking for a part-time modern foreign language teacher since one of the two part-timers that were hired to replace me had already left. Now, I was facing a dilemma. Did I want to go back to the place where all my stress and anxiety of failing started, despite the fact that it was only a part-time position in a school that I already knew? I wasn't sure. After discussing with my husband, who I thought would obviously try to convince me to apply for the post (which he did not as he recalled how unhappy I was in the end), I decided to go for it. If it was meant to be it would happen anyway, we thought. So, I submitted my application and within a couple of days, I received the invitation for an interview. Thinking back, I consider this move one of my bigger mistakes, however at that time, I was quite excited about having been invited. It gave me a sense of achievement and acknowledgement after months of dealing with a crying baby at night, dirty nappies, and neglecting my personal needs. Once I had confirmed my attendance for the interview and was given further details regarding the class and topic I had to teach, I knuckled down to prepare my interview lesson. I found myself to be quite nervous. It's been a long time since I had taught a lesson to a class full of secondary school kids. Was I able to deliver the lesson that was a good one on paper? Will I still be able to stand in front of a classroom of 30 children? What will the behaviour be like; any different from what I knew? And the biggest question of all was: Can I do justice to the expectations the observers, especially the Head of Department will have? I pushed away all these thoughts somehow until the day of the interview. Nervously, I made my way to the school. When I arrived, it felt good to be greeted by familiar faces who were telling me how good it was to see me. Everything felt so comfortable. That is until I stepped into the Headmaster's office for his welcome. Luckily, I wasn't alone. The two other candidates were there, too. It wouldn't have been a big deal, if only the Headmaster hadn't tried to sell my re-applying as a plus point for the school. "The fact that Lalita wants to join our school again speaks for itself", he said. This made me realise that in reality, I didn't want to be there. As it is very often, my instincts knew that this was not the right place for me to be, but my head was just about to understand. After the Headmaster's welcome, I was taken to the student council, a new addition to the interview process. A bunch of students sat there in front of me asking me very mature questions. I didn't know whether I found it nice to see former students of mine or awkward having to answer their sometimes very deep questions. This was not the strangest part, though. In fact, I thought that I managed this very well. When the children entered the classroom for my interview lesson, that's when the whole experience started to reveal itself as a big stupid mistake, finally, to my brain. I was stumbling my way through the lesson like an unqualified beginner and sensed the pressure of being observed by people that I knew, just like I had expected. I was so glad when the lesson was over and could already tell that this was not going to be a successful one. After every candidate had delivered their lessons, we were waiting outside the Headmaster's office again. This time, we were waiting for the verdict. I knew it was just the normal interview procedure that only the successful person would be called in, but when I was sent home without even any feedback or a casual word from the Headmaster, to whom I shouldn't have been just any candidate since he knew me and I had worked there for a year (at least I thought), I felt fooled with, yet again. I went home being highly disappointed, not because I didn't get the job, but because I applied for it, went to the interview and got turned down in a manner that didn't seem right to me, given the fact that I used to be a member of staff. Now I know that I had too high expectations. Why would they treat me nicely or even care about me if they didn't need me? For me, that was it. I was not going to apply for any other teaching job anymore. I was done with it. In my job-search, I completely blocked out teaching positions and, in the end, I went for a job as a coffee shop barista on a zero-hours contract in a service-centre on a motorway.

My family wasn't too keen that I took on a job that I was overqualified for. They kept asking why I hurried so much to go back to work. The answer was: I didn't want to sit at home, being stuck in the same routine and I missed my old self that was active and financially independent. I wanted to contribute to the family's expenses and to be able to buy my son things out of my own pocket. At that stage, to me, any job was better than being a teacher. All I wanted was to go to work, do my job, earn some money, come back home and not have to think about work anymore. The barista job seemed just perfect as I had done something similar before in Germany when I was a teenager.

I received some training about the company, their products and vision and I was ready to go and be a barista. I was quite happy making coffee and other beverages for the folks that stopped at the service centre during their journey that day. It was a change seeing new faces every day and I could even show off my language skills when German or French customers came along. Being a mother of a seven-month-old who would still wake up at night, decide to fall asleep late, or to wake up early, the working hours were a little inconvenient sometimes. Plus, I had to work most weekends, when everybody else in the family had their days off, so that I missed some of the fun and the outings. I became especially envious when my husband or other family members took out my little one while I was at work. It made me feel like a bad mother who preferred to work instead of spending time with her baby. And of course, I really missed him during my shifts. So, secretly, I was content when it was raining and everybody just stayed at home being bored and watching TV. A few months passed and a strange feeling had gradually set in. I couldn't put my finger on it, but something felt not quite right about going to work anymore. I wasn't as motivated and happy as I was when I started the job. Certain things began to irritate me and some of the customers annoyed me by being overly dramatic about their coffee. Often, when a customer behaved unnecessarily difficult and demanding about their beverage, I thought to myself "It is JUST coffee, why are you making such a fuss?!". And there it was. It was just coffee that I was making. This is not what I ever wanted to do for a living. I wanted to shape lives and contribute to the future of the society. What was I doing behind a big coffee machine? I was making coffee for random people who sometimes assumed and implied that I was uneducated and stupid for standing behind the bar. I served people whom I would never see again in my life and who would not remember me for anything. I realised that I was betraying myself and that I couldn't carry on like this. I remembered that I have always wanted to do something meaningful which is why I wanted to become a teacher. With this realisation, I gathered all my courage and decided to start looking for teaching positions again.

8. My come-back

It was meant to be

I had barely decided to get back on the teaching track when an opportunity presented itself very unexpectedly. My former mentor and friend tagged me in a Facebook post. A teacher had advertised a maternity cover position at a school in London for herself. She was going on leave in November and the languages department were urgently looking for her replacement. The funny thing was, my friend didn't even know that I had been thinking of going back to teaching again. It was mere coincidence that she tagged me in that post, but it seemed as if it was meant to be. So, I thanked my friend for the tagging and contacted the teacher who had made the post. She responded very quickly, giving me a few more details about the school and the Head of Department's email address, to whom I was supposed to send a covering letter and a CV. Soon after I sent my email to the Head of MFL of that school, she came back to me asking me to fill out the school's job application form and also invited me for an interview. For some reason, I had a very good feeling about this interview and about how things were going with regards to this opportunity in general. It all just had a positive vibe to it and I felt very confident that I would get the job. I sensed some kind of maturity and experience inside of me that I never noticed before. I secretly prepared for the interview as I didn't want anybody apart from my husband to know about it. I wanted to avoid anybody having high expectations and then being disappointed. The day before the interview, I just told my mother-in-law that I had a meeting at my workplace the next day. So, in the morning, I left the house, feeling positive and proud of myself for attending this interview and trying to seize what seemed like a good opportunity.

When I arrived at the school, there was one single parking spot that was free in front of the admin building, the "Manor House", as if it was reserved for me. I couldn't use the staff parking on the other side of the school premises as I would need a batch for the barrier to open. So I parked my car and went inside. The Manor House was an old building with creaky floorboards. When I reported at reception, I was told to take a seat on one of the chairs on the side and wait for the Head of Department. A few minutes into waiting, a tall and slim woman approached me, introducing herself as Claire. She took me on a tour around the school and introduced me to the other members of the department, including the colleague who was about to go on maternity leave. After the tour, I was brought to the classroom where I was supposed to teach my lesson to a group of Year 8 students. I had to teach the topic of music genres in German, which I felt very comfortable with and I could sense that the lesson was going well, too. I noticed a certain maturity and experience inside of me, which I credited to the many interviews I had been to before and the year of teaching that I had already behind me. I knew what the observing teachers would want to see and hear and the fact that I did was so strange to me at that time. I had never felt so confident before and was quite proud of myself, regardless of whether I would be successful or not. After the lesson, the usual interview conversation with the Head of department, her line manager, who was also a language teacher and a school governor took place. Again, I seemed to have just the right feeling of how I had to respond to the questions thrown at me. Afterwards, I was told to wait outside where I sat after checking in on my arrival that morning. While waiting, the good feeling that I was having all along stuck with me. Eventually, the other young candidate who was in the conference room before me came out and headed towards the exit straight away. At that moment, I was not quite sure what to think. Either, they did not like any of us or I actually convince them. I was called inside the second I had taken a seat, the line manager began to glow at me and announced that they would like to offer me the job. The obvious response at that time for me was to accept the offer. I was over the moon that I managed to get back on track after having a baby and not having taught in school for more than a year. This small success gave me a sense of accomplishment and the confidence that I was wanted, a sought after asset in the world of teaching. Never would I have imagined that my time at this school would cause me a physical and mental trauma that would be difficult to overcome even several years later. That day I went home being very proud of myself and satisfied that I would be financially independent again. Of course my husband and the rest of the family were happy about this accomplishment, although everyone, including me, was a little nervous about how it was all going to work out with our son. My mother-in-law has always been a home-maker, so she was going to be at home with our little one and take care of him, but the question was whether he would adapt to the new situation and be fine with it. Either way, we had no choice as we needed the money and I desperately wanted to go back to work.

All is well

So, I started my new position at the beginning of November. My timetable was very light as I was replacing the Head of German, Charlotte. Her responsibility allowed her to have more free lessons to fulfil her tasks and so I was lucky to just inherit her schedule except without the additional duties. I was even allowed to use the lessons that Charlotte had created and saved in the shared area of the language department. This came in extremely handy for me as someone who was just getting back into the profession while raising a child. I barely had to prepare anything, so that it gave me a lot of time after work to spend with my little one, who at that time had just turned one. I would only plan the occasional lesson from scratch if I didn't know how to teach Charlotte's PowerPoint or if I simply didn't like it. My other colleagues all seemed very nice and happy to have me in their team. There was Grace, the newly qualified teacher for German and Spanish with whom I clicked right from the start, Emily who taught French and Spanish, and Beth who mainly taught French and Spanish as well. On the whole, this new position gave me a sense of fulfilment as I felt welcomed, I was doing what I loved for a living while contributing to the financial household as well as enjoying quality time with my son and family. Furthermore, I was coaching two student teachers who were completing their placements at the school. It was a gratifying experience as I could give the trainees valuable tips that came from my time as a trainee teacher and seeing them trying to incorporate my advice into their lessons and improving things was rewarding. On top of that, I had to prepare for even fewer lessons as long as the trainee teachers were there. One of them, Dave, was making good progress and we connected on a personal level, maybe because, like Grace, he was about my age. It was fun working and chatting with him. In addition, he had lived and worked in Germany before wanting to become a teacher in England, so we had a lot to talk about. The other trainee was called Sylvie. She was a middle-aged woman who found it challenging to handle the computer and connect with the students. She had trouble planning lessons on her own so that Emily and I would spend a lot of time with her going through ideas with her after school. Although I was able to leave work straight after the end of lessons on most days in the first few months, I missed quite a few baby moments of our little one which made me somewhat emotional from time to time. In fact, I was on edge most of the time and noticed some symptoms in my body that I could not explain. My husband kept telling me that I was extremely irritable and that he had to walk on egg-shells around me as anything, even the most insignificant comment or event could upset me. I came to the realisation that I was not being myself and that I had to do something about it. I thought to see a connection between my physical symptoms and the way I behaved, so we went to see our GP. Ultimately, I was diagnosed with mild post-natal depression and a CBT (cognitive behavioural therapy) course was prescribed for me. Privately and internally, I was going through a rough time. Strangely and luckily, somehow I was able to keep work out of it completely. School was my safe place although I sometimes had to deal with difficult students in my Year 9 Set 5 French class, who even managed to make me cry, although one of the trainees taught most of their lessons. Also, I was always nervous about whether I was preparing my Year 11 German GCSE class well for their final exams. Despite all the dramatic and annoying moments at school, I loved going there whereas going home after work was the difficult part, although I had the love of my life waiting for me at home, eager to smile at me and call me his mummy. I started the CBT class in mid-January and went there straight after work for two months. It was a bit of a drive and those days were very long, dark, and cold in every sense. At home, except for my husband, everyone thought that I had meetings. We both agreed that we didn't want to make anyone worry and I partially thought that nobody would understand my problem and why I was having to go to these classes anyway. So, we kept it a secret. Making the long way from school to the CBT class paid off as after a couple of months it felt as I was reborn. I had a whole new perspective on life and had regained my self-confidence. It didn't change much for me at work but it was nice to recognise myself in the mirror again. One day, when I was quietly pondering about random things in my classroom while marking some tests, Claire, my Head of Department, entered and wished to talk to me for a minute. She started off by asking whether I had any plans after my maternity cover ended at the end of the term. I said that I wanted to look for another job and stay employed in the field of education, but that I didn't have any concrete plans. Upon that she asked me a question that I did not expect but that apparently I had been waiting for. Claire wanted to know if I would like to stay at the school and become a permanent member of the staff. I didn't have to think twice, but I was so overwhelmed and happy that I started tearing up and funnily so was Claire when I responded with a 'yes' and said that I was feeling so comfortable and as if I was at the right place. When I asked her how this was even possible, Claire revealed that she was 12 weeks pregnant and that her classes needed to be covered the next term. She explained that after that she wants to keep me as a member of the department and that she would plead for the department's teaching hours to be distributed in a way that I could have an amount of lessons which it would be worth staying for. To me, it sounded like a solid plan and I was still over the moon that I was asked to stay at the school after the maternity cover, which was the cherry on top for me that year. I felt like finally having found the right place for me to work at and that things were going to be okay. On top, I was going to be the new supervisor for the subject of French in the upcoming term. It sounded very fancy and important and as if I could make some creative contributions back then. It was sold to me and my colleague and friend Grace as being a tiny job on the side, where we would have to stay at school an extra half an hour, occasionally. We only found out later what it actually was: being the assistant of the acting head of department and doing all the work she didn't have the time for. It was basically a delegation of her responsibilities and we had little say in any matter. However, more on this subject in the next chapter.

Being made a permanent member of staff and appointed to the supervisor of French not only meant for me that I was doing well at my job but also that I was getting better at it, which gave me a big confidence-boost. For the first time, I was going to come back to the same school after the holidays. On the one hand I was excited as I wouldn't have to get used to a new environment again, but on the other hand I was nervous about whether I would have to rise up to higher expectations and whether I could do it. I was suppressing the latter thought and focused on being happy about all my achievements. When I sat in the end of term staff gathering where speeches were held for those leaving the school, I thought to myself that this was not going to happen to me in the near future. I was planning on staying at this school for a longer time, making progress on the career ladder and becoming a tenured member of the school's teaching staff. So, having finished the term on a positive note, I went home looking forward to six weeks of relaxing and catching up on quality time with my family.

In August, I went back to school for results day to see how the Year 11 boys that I had taken over from Charlotte did in their German exams. When I got there, Charlotte was already waiting, while rocking her baby girl to sleep. We were both excited to find out the boys' German grades. It turned out that we were more excited than them. When they opened their envelopes, almost none of them seemed to care about the German result. They didn't even look at it at first and when they saw it, the response was rather indifferent. Even the ones who were (or pretended to be?) enthusiastic and did very well in lessons didn't bother much about it, despite the very good outcomes. Charlotte and I were amongst the very few teachers that had come to be there for the boys when they received one of the most important piece of paper of their lives, but we were hardly noticed or given any gratitude. I think what I expected was some sort of relief or joy from the students' side and that they shared it with us. I felt disappointment rising inside myself when I noticed that the boys didn't care and most of them left without a word to us German teachers. Sadly, this showed me, once again, that despite the importance that the school might place on modern foreign languages, the students don't give it much, if any significance. Confused about what to think of results day, I returned home where I quickly pushed aside any negative thoughts that started to arise and enjoyed another two weeks of holidays.

9. The beginning of the end

The gut never lies

The new term started with an INSET day. Claire was on maternity leave now and Emily, with whom I got along very well in the previous term, was the acting Head of Department for the term. I was very excited to be back at the same school for a new term and to be an actual part of the languages crew.

The INSET day began quite relaxed with breakfast and it was nice to see all the colleagues after the long summer break. Everyone seemed refreshed and well rested and that's how I felt, too. It didn't take long though, until this state of mind and body vanished. After breakfast, everyone headed to their departments. I don't remember what exactly we did that day. All I can recall is that tasks for the new term were discussed (including how to make sure that GCSE results in the languages department became better that year. Especially now that Claire was on maternity leave and we were one woman down, we had to prove ourselves) and that I didn't quite like what was happening, especially inside of me. A very strange feeling of anxiety and being overwhelmed started to creep up. I tried to remain calm and confident but my body was shaking as if I had the shivers. My colleague Grace felt a similar way and we both brushed it off as a normal feeling of still being quite new to the school and also having to fulfil a few new tasks. In retrospect I would say that the gut feeling that I had at that time was right and that my body was trying to tell me what my mind only realised later on: the pressure was on. After the resignation of the previous Headmaster, they tried to find a successor. None of the candidates seemed to convince the board of governors so that one of the deputy head teachers became the Head teacher with the beginning of the new term. However, not only did we have a new Head teacher, we basically had a new head of everything, at least a lot. Many teachers were promoted into a leadership position. The newly gained influence and position somehow seemed to mean that they had to prove themselves. It felt like everyone was micromanaging someone below them in the hierarchy. The last ones in the chain, us teachers, were the ones who had to endure all the pressure that was coming from all sides. We had to constantly perform so that our heads of departments would look good in front of their line managers, as those again had to make an impression on the leadership team. It was all a vicious cycle and there was no escape from the pressure unless you rose up to be one of the people who exercised pressure on others. A theory I once heard from someone is that most teachers remain in their jobs and manage the pressure as well as the imbalance between work and life because they secure themselves a leadership position. They either take on a higher post in their subject department or in the pastoral sector, e.g. become head of year. It is true that even heads and leaders are victims of micromanaging and pressure, however, they do not have to deal with student behaviour, lessons, and parents. The new leadership structures brought a strange atmosphere over the school and its staff. Everyone seemed to be more tense than usual and it was noticeable very soon after the term had begun. But not only the teachers were behaving differently. The boys who were still childish mentally, had grown to become physically more mature giants over the summer. Nearly every student looked as if he had drunk a growth potion and their voices had changed, too. Especially, the boys from my previous Year 8 French class, who were now in year 9, seemed to have gone through a growth spurt over the summer. Some children who were just a few inches taller or even the same height as me the previous term, I had to suddenly look up at. I got to almost feel their strength in the second week of term. Two very tall and hefty Year 9 boys were having a fight right in front of my classroom during break time. They were holding each other's throats and locked eyes with one another. I taught one of them and the other one I've only seen around in school. I felt it was my duty to break up the fight. I yelled at them several times to let go of each other and tried to pull them apart, but it was a futile attempt. They didn't even seem to notice that I was there. Around us were a bunch of other boys of the same year group shouting several things, towards the fighting boys or to each other. One of the two took a swing in order to actually beat the other one. It was only a matter of a split second; if I hadn't moved my head away in a blink of an eye, I would have been hit severely in my face. Neither I nor the other boy met the fist and the situation de-escalated when I realised that I wasn't able to achieve anything and, still in shock, sent another bystander to get the deputy head of year, James, whose office was just on one end of the corridor. Once he arrived, all the boys seemed to have dispersed, even the two who were fighting. I was waiting in my classroom and the class that I should have been teaching was directed to Beth's classroom so that she could take over for me. When James came to see me, I was still processing the fact that I was almost hit by a student. He asked me what had happened and I explained that one of the boys was aiming for the other and almost hit me. At least that's what I thought I said because when the Head teacher spoke to me a few minutes later, it turned out that the message had been conveyed wrongly. He had heard that the boy was aiming for me, which would have been a very serious issue and could lead to suspension. I assured that it was none of the boys' intention to beat me and that it was my idea to go in between them and stop the fight that they were having. The Head teacher praised my efforts and my objective to break up the fight, but he also said that I didn't have to do this. He strongly recommended staying out of boy fights in the future given the fact that I am petite. According to him, there was no harm in protecting myself and just sending a student to get a member of staff who is taller and stronger, which made sense to me. I just couldn't figure out at that time why the boys were so unapproachable and why they just wouldn't let go of each other although an adult was yelling at them to stop. I was told that when boys fight, it's all about the fight and the amount of testosterone in their veins at that time probably won't allow them to think straight. I don't know if that's the truth but to this day, I am glad that I didn't have to have my glasses replaced or my face mended. However, this event seemed to have set the tone for the rest of the term for me. I was hoping that the term would only get better from then on, but my hopes should not be fulfilled.

As I got to know my classes over the next few weeks, it dawned on me that It was going to be a very tough school year. I had four Year 9 classes, my form that I was covering for Claire, a German set and a French set which I also had taken over from Claire and Emily, as well as my previous French class. Apart from those, I also had my own Year 11 group that I had taught the previous term and who needed to be prepared for their GCSE exams in German, a Year 7 German class, a Year 8 French class, and not to forget my Year 13 A-Level German class. Nevertheless, I had a feeling that the Year 9 students would cost me every drop of energy that I had and unfortunately, I was right. For three Year 9 classes out of four, I was new and on top of that the children, who were innocent little boys before, were now pubescent teenagers and behaved in a way that I found difficult to deal with. They were constantly testing their boundaries, not only with their teachers but also with each other. It seemed as if they had to do certain things in order to prove their masculinity. It was always loud around them and I realised that I was missing the girls. I have to admit that I despised seeing my form every single morning and the thought of having to deal with the trouble they were causing in their classes and around the school made my stomach turn. Obviously, not every single student was badly behaved, however the ones who were giving me a hard time did it in a way that it overshadowed the good things other students did. Looking back, I don't know how I survived that term, but I didn't come out of it without long-term consequences for my body, mind and soul. It wasn't just the students who were pushing me, but also the acting Head of

Department and the school system itself took everything and more than I could deliver out of me. But let me give you an impression of each Year 9 class individually.

9W

Let's begin with my form. This bunch of boys was known to be one of the more challenging groups. One boy named Rowley, who was hardly there but caused problems when he was, either insulted fellow students or members of staff or bunked lessons that he didn't like going to. At the beginning of the term, when I was still new to the boys, he kept challenging me every time he was there. One day, he started creepily hanging around by my classroom door during break time and just looked at me. When I told him to go outside as it was break, he would just ignore me and keep staring. At first, I tried to take no notice of him when he was bumming around my classroom, but when he started inviting himself into the room without my permission, I mentioned it to the Head of Year, Kim. Bottom line, Rowley was told to stay away from me and my classroom when there was no reason to be there. On top of his weird and creepy behaviour, he was not a healthy boy. He had health issues and often his poor conduct would be excused on the basis of this fact. Of course the only logical consequence would be to misbehave or swear around and the teachers had to just deal with it. I might be exaggerating here, but this is what happened in a nutshell.

Another boy who was giving me a hell of a time was Jordan. Funnily enough, he wasn't very conspicuous at the beginning. However, when he noticed that I wouldn't let him just sleep or talk continuously during form time or German lessons, he seemed to have decided to make it his mission to just ignore any of my instructions, reprimands, and me. He didn't do or say much that was as terrible as what came from other students, but the fact that he had the guts to not move his finger to write down a single word during a one-hour lesson, to pretend I wasn't there at all or to tell me to leave him alone, to go away or that he didn't want to talk to me because he didn't like me made my blood boil. I had to email his father, who was a single dad, quite often. When no strategy to address Jordan's behaviour and attitude seemed to work, I had to schedule a meeting with him and his father. Kim advised me to send out an email to all of Jordan's teachers to gather some information about his behaviour, attitude and work in other lessons in order to back up my case when meeting with the dad. Not only was this a good way of gathering evidence, but it also demonstrated that I was not the only teacher Jordan was playing up with. Looking at my colleagues' feedback, I realised that Jordan was having trouble participating and staying respectful towards his teachers across the board. Especially with his English teacher he seemed to have difficult situations quite frequently. There were only one or two colleagues who said that his work was alright but a little more effort and positive attitude would be good. The best part was that I could just present Jordan's father a printout of all the feedback that I received, when he subtly suggested that there must be something that I was doing so that Jordan would be reacting in a certain way. After all, he never had problems with his former tutor, Claire, and he "used to love German", also with Claire. When he read the teachers' comments, he looked baffled. It was obvious that Jordan's father was in the belief that everything was going well for his son and that it was me, his tutor and German teacher, who was blowing things out of proportion and doing things to trigger Jordan. It was only when dad was reading the sheet that he realised that things weren't going well at all. He apologised for the trouble Jordan had been causing and then turned to his son to ask what was going on. Jordan's eyes filled with tears but he insisted that everything was fine. An argument between father and son commenced but quickly settled. Both Kim and I, assured Jordan that we were there for him whatever was on his mind, but made it clear that he had to change his ways of talking to and behaving towards his teachers. I, for my part, stressed to both, father and son, that it was not my intention for Jordan to like me or be his favourite teacher but that I was his tutor at the end of the day and that it was my duty to be a point of contact for him. Unfortunately, or fortunately, I had to leave to get to my lesson on time but the meeting continued for a few more minutes according to Kim. Basically, Jordan was having a hard time privately. Apparently, there was some girl he liked and went out with but then she broke up which affected his ego and confidence. To be honest, I couldn't care less. Not because I didn't care about my students, but because I was sick and tired of students and parents who thought that whatever was going on in their lives, they could just bring it to school and dump it on their teachers. Don't get me wrong, of course there are things that will affect a child's behaviour and mood, consequently their performance and conduct in school. These could be death, parents' divorce, illness of a close family member, etc., you get the gist. However, telling me about other problems that are caused by puberty and presenting them as an excuse for poor attitude towards school staff triggered me. It seemed that the majority of kids were taught that they didn't have to put up with anything they didn't like and that they were responsible to no one or didn't have to obey anyone. Only their feelings counted and they could just let it out whenever and wherever... Anyways, Jordan's attitude improved after our meeting and we managed to maintain a relationship that was based on distance and fulfilment of basic requirements. I didn't try to maintain a (tutor-tutee) relationship with him, but performed my duties as his tutor when he was in need, while he tried his best to meet core expectations.

Then, there was Jake. Jake caused me so much trouble that I had to put in a considerable amount of effort in order to control my anger. He was a ticking time bomb. He would never stay in his seat and he'd be constantly irritating his classmates. You never knew what new stupid thing he was up to almost every single day. It was like being in a sanctuary when he was absent. I somehow managed to calm Jake down in form time by giving him break time detentions every single time he spoke or did something out of line. Unfortunately, it cost me many break times that I would have loved to spend alone, but at least it helped me to gain his attention. However, it did not help with his behaviour in other lessons, where he would constantly get into trouble. As if that wasn't enough and despite my strict take on his conduct, Jake got me into a very difficult situation that would cost me a lot of energy and some sleepless nights.

Usually, before form time began, I would do some last-minute preparation and printing for my classes that day. It could become quite stressful when most of the students had already arrived as I had to keep an eye on them while trying to get ready for my lessons (because I didn't want to and couldn't work until past midnight). I had to divide my attention and one day, it had to get out of control. While I was looking at my computer screen and listening to the boys' conversations, I seemed to have missed that a major fight was cooking up in the middle of the classroom. To this day, I don't understand how I could have missed out on it, but it must have started very subtly with Jake constantly annoying and irritating a classmate called Theo. Theo was usually a rather quiet and well-behaved boy, who occasionally got carried away in chats with his mates, but was one of the students who were accountable for the good things that happened in this group. He was always very polite and exuded a sense of calm. Yet, he demonstrated his other side when he was pushed to his boundaries by Jake's silly activities. One minute, I was quietly working on a worksheet, the next I heard shouting and roaring from the boys. I jumped from my chair to get whatever happened under control, but I was shocked to discover that it was already too late. Theo had given Jake a clout with a chair. Some kids were left in consternation; others were amused by the events. For me, the whole situation was too much to handle, especially because I didn't see it coming as I was not fully (mentally) there. I could sense that this was going to become a big deal and at that time, I didn't know how to deal with it. The first thing I did was to take Jake and Theo outside the classroom. I made another boy go and get James, the Deputy Head of Year. In the meantime, while the mob was going crazy inside the classroom, I tried to speak to the boys outside. Looking back at the whole situation, I know that I could have managed it better if I had stayed calm, but as I said, I was overwhelmed. When Theo tried to defend himself and explain what he did, which was in no way a justifiable reaction, I barely listened. I raised my voice against him and didn't even care to ask or listen to why it had come to this point. All I could see and understand was that Theo had hit Jake with a chair and that he was in pain. While Jake just sat on the floor, complaining how much his head hurt, Theo was clearly upset about the whole situation. His eyes were teary and he made a very long face. A couple of minutes after I had gone back inside to take care of the rest of the class, James arrived and was speaking to the two outside. Theo was sent back into the room and Jake was taken to be picked up and to stay at home in case he turned out to have a concussion. When Theo came inside, I was in the middle of giving an angry speech to my form. Thinking back, I am convinced that I shouldn't have continued to make this incident a topic. I was emotionally loaded, which made me say stupid things like: "There are some, who are perfectly behaved and do everything right but don't get enough credit because most of you in this class behave like di**-heads!" There it was. At that time, I honestly didn't know that the word "di**-head" is a very pejorative and vulgar word to say that someone is very stupid and dumb. I was so naïve to believe that it just meant something like "Dummkopf" in German, which could be translated into 'idiot' or 'goof' and is obviously a less insulting expression. The second I said it, I saw a change of expression in the boys' faces and sensed a weird vibe in the room. That's when I knew that I obviously had said something inappropriate. At first I thought that the students probably would have forgotten about all this once they left the classroom. I didn't even mention my little outburst to Kim or James. In my eyes, it wasn't relevant and it wasn't necessary for everyone to know everything that I did or said. The fact that I had used the word "dickhead" in front of a bunch of teenagers caused me issues in the end. I felt the need to share my guilt feelings with Kim and James as soon as Theo's mother emailed me and asked to speak to me over the phone. In private, I told each of the Year 9 Heads that this word slipped out of my mouth in a moment of anger and that I knew that it was very unprofessional. They both assured me that it happens and that I shouldn't beat myself up for it. At the same time, Kim revealed that she knew about this before because some parent had complained about it. She thought that it wouldn't serve me knowing this and also, she wanted to see if I would ever confess. When I called Theo's mother, James sat next to me in order to provide moral support, in case she became difficult. The conversation was indeed one of the more challenging ones that I had to lead in my career as a teacher. Bottom line, the mother wanted to know how I, as their form tutor and the responsible adult in that room, didn't see it coming that a major incident was going to happen. Honestly, I didn't have an answer. Since I was struggling with a guilty conscience myself, this question hit me pretty hard. I tried to talk myself out of it by saying that it all happened really fast and that I saw something from the corner of my eye but when I wanted to intervene it was already too late.

Of course, this was not the truth. In reality, I was focused on getting my lessons ready for the day and didn't sense one bit that violence was cooking up inside the classroom. Theo's mother kept insisting that I must have noticed and should have done something to prevent the incident from happening. She was right, hundred percent. But what was I supposed to do about it now? It happened and there was nothing I could do about it. That drove me crazy. The woman insisted that the other boy was punished, too, as he provoked Theo until he reacted the way he did. James, who was listening all along, nodded signalling that this would be done. So, I assured her that "the other boy", Jake, was being dealt with. After this phone conversation, I was very exhausted and all the anxiety and stress that I had built up beforehand were released through tears. I went home thinking that this matter was now closed, especially because the lady hadn't brought up my little slip of tongue. Relief started to settle in until I saw the appointment list for the Year 9 parents' evening. It seemed as if Theo's mother wasn't quite finished with me as yet. She made it a priority to come and see me at parents' evening. "Another horrible Year 9 parents' meeting I'm having to experience", I thought to myself. This time, the mother brought support. Theo's father came along. One could tell by just looking at his face that he was very unhappy. His face was as if it was made of stone. He didn't make a single other facial expression than the one he had at the beginning of our meeting, a frown. Throughout the meeting, it was him who was asking all the questions that I had already dealt with during the phone call. He was more persistent with his opinion that I failed as a tutor when the incident with Theo and Jake happened. I shouldn't have let it come to this point and it was inexplicable to him how I could. And then, there it was: they both found it very unprofessional, with justification, that I was swearing at the kids afterwards. According to the parents, Theo was feeling extremely vulnerable and guilty after he had hit Jake with a chair and I made it worse by calling him and the class "dickheads". I kept stressing how sorry I was, how it had been bothering me that I had used these kinds of words in front of my tutees, and that it would never happen again. However, no matter what I said, Theo's parents didn't seem to be convinced. The father hadn't changed his face throughout the whole conversation and the mother kept circling back to her point that I shouldn't have let this happen. I didn't seem to get any understanding, let alone mercy whatsoever. So, I just said that the incident and everything around it happened, that there was nothing we could do about it now, and that it was something to learn from for all of us, especially me. I said that we were dealing with the other boy and that we are doing everything possible to solve the situation. Finally, after my dead-end response to their whining, the moment I was longing for since their arrival came and they were ready to move on to their next appointment, which was with Kim, the Head of Year. The whole experience left me with yet another mental scar. I completely agreed with everything that Theo's parents said. What annoyed me and somehow fagged me out was the fact that they couldn't let go. They couldn't accept the fact that after all it was their son, who had smacked someone with a chair, and they couldn't accept the fact that I, as a teacher, was only human after all. And I believe that this is a major problem in the day-to-day school life. Teachers don't seem to be regarded as humans with their own emotions, strengths and weaknesses, private problems, let alone personalities. They are treated as machines that are supposed to teach children not only their subjects but also manners and acceptable behaviour because modern parents don't seem to have the time or motivation to do that at home. Teachers are also expected to cater to the students' every need and to listen to every inappropriate thing they had to say to them. Bottom line, the teacher is supposed to take all responsibility for what the student does or doesn't do. The teacher is not human, but a machine with a thick skin that prepares lessons only to be sabotaged by inappropriately behaved kids. The teacher is a machine that doesn't have emotions and can endure any kind of insults from students and parents. The teacher doesn't have a personality and thus can be stipulated how to teach, as only one way is the right way. The teacher doesn't have a life and therefore can be completing an unimaginable amount of admin work or post-processing after the school day. The teacher doesn't work with the student but for the student.

These were the thoughts occupying my mind after the meeting with Theo's parents and I still believe them to be true for many

English school settings. I had gathered enough and was to gather more experience that confirmed my assumptions above.

You see, my form was a handful. I was told that my class was one of the more challenging forms amongst the year group. Unfortunately, I barely had the time to devote to the quieter and well-achieving students in that group due to a few boys. They managed to overshadow the good things that happened in that class and being around them drained me of energy. On top of this very high-maintenance tutor group, I also had to deal with other Year 9 classes of which I am going to talk about in the next section.

Year 9 Overload

When it comes to class distribution, I couldn't have had a worse allocation of classes in that school term. The majority of my timetable was filled with Year 9 lessons. It wouldn't have bothered me so much, if it had been classes with good kids who were willing to learn, such as in Set 1 or 2. However, I had to put up with two Set 3 classes, one in French and one in German and one Set 4 class in French. The problem with Set 3 classes was that most kids could have done better but chose not to. They chose to put the very bare minimum of effort into their work and most of them had no desire to do better. It was the comfortable mediocre place between the two "upper" and the two "lower" sets. For the teacher this meant that they had to try and motivate the students to do better and teach them the more complex stuff in an easier way while dealing with a lot of nuisance. I can't even begin to describe the aggravation the few boys in my German class caused me during lessons. There were especially two little devils who literally made my life hell. One of them was called Oliver. Oliver was a teenager who had the ability to destabilise you with every word and action that came from him. He sat right in front of me but what I got to see the most of him was his back as he was constantly turned around to the person behind him and chatting. When, after asking him politely to turn around for the hundredth time, I wanted to put him in his place, he vigorously contested that he had ever turned around or talked. He would neither leave the room when I asked him to, because according to him he hadn't done anything, nor come to the detentions I set him. After a while I got him to stop turning around so much. Instead, he now continuously blabbered something or made silly noises. He commented on every single thing that I said or did, even if it didn't concern him at all. And again, when telling him to cease the behaviour, he made a huge scene either claiming he had never said anything or that he was "just humming because [he was] in a good mood". There was no winning with Oliver. If I wanted to deliver a somewhat okay lesson, he couldn't be in the class. Oliver was the kind of boy who had the ability to make you lose your self-control. He could aggravate you so much that you couldn't help but want to just grab him by his collar and shake him till his teeth rattled. As for me, he pushed it so far that the mere sight of him made my blood boil. I had emailed his mum and spoke to her couple of times about his conduct and the fact that he rarely brought his German material, to top it all off. Each time, she pointed out that Oliver didn't have any problems in other lessons and that I was the only teacher telling her all these things about her son. At the end of the conversations she told me to make a note in Oliver's school journal if there was an issue. Each time I wrote a message to Oliver's mum in his journal, it came back signed off and that was it. Nothing that I did or said had any effect on him whatsoever. So, I decided to deprive him of what he apparently needed the most, attention. I tried to completely ignore him. When he behaved or spoke out of line, I didn't even say a word to him but just wrote his name on the board. When he contested, I pretended that he didn't exist. In short, I gave him the silent treatment. This clearly wasn't to his liking. When he realised that I didn't attend to him, no matter how much he disrupted the lesson, he became offended. That, on the other hand, turned out to be even more unbearable and a bigger nuisance than his other nonsense. Either way, I was between a rock and a hard place. I made an agreement with Charlotte that, as soon as Oliver's behaviour became intolerable again, I would send him to her room, where she was either teaching the top set of Oliver's year group or some older students. It was supposed to intimidate him a little, but it didn't seem like it was working. It seemed like that boy only came to school to sit out his time, make his teachers' lives hell and go to detentions. At least that's what I thought. Sometimes, I felt sorry for him as he didn't even seem to have real friends. In my eyes, you either go to school in order to learn or to be with your friends, or both. But if none of these apply, I really don't know what a child could be aiming for by going to school. Anyways, my feeling sorry for Oliver would never last very long. There was no way of reasoning with him. He wouldn't take anything serious and there wasn't anything serious about him. When I tried to have a word with him, one on one, without any students around, and find a common ground or come to some sort of accordance with him, it was an effort in vain. Anything I said, he blocked it off or made a joke of it. In the end, as I said, I would just send him away. Out of sight, out of mind, I thought.

That didn't mean that all my problems in that German class were solved as soon as Oliver wasn't in the room anymore. Another boy called William was at least as annoying as Oliver. The only difference between their behaviour was that Oliver wouldn't be offended when I sent him out and it was the only command he obeyed. Whereas William always had to make a huge scene when I wanted him out because he had been fooling around and distracting everyone around him. According to him, I was always picking on him and discriminating him. At times, he refused to step out and had to be picked up by the teacher on on-call duty and put into Charlotte's room, although it was just across mine. William, as opposed to Oliver, brought his material, but the sight of it made me think why even bother. When Oliver was rude in a sly and indirect way and always had a smirk on his face, William was very direct and aggressive. He would start swearing and make blunt insults. Consequently, there was a meeting with his father, or should I say step-father. It came to light that William had a lot going on at home. Apparently, he was as rude to his parents and also seemed to have an addiction to an online game. He was sleep-deprived and on top of that pubescent. The step-father seemed very supportive and assured that he, more than William's mother, was really trying hard to make him understand that this is not the way to behave in school or anywhere. He promised that he would tackle this with William but asked us, me and the Heads of Year, to be patient but consistent. He would have our backs. It was nice to see a parent who was aware of their child's attitude and behaviour for a change. It really helps the student (and the teachers) when teachers and parents pull in the same direction. Over the course of the weeks, I could see a change in William's conduct. I could actually access him and reason with him. Sometimes, he had set-backs and in combination with everything else that would go on in that class (I have only presented to you the three most prominent students), lessons were catastrophic. I decided to just endure the class, as Charlotte, contrary to Emily, told me to just make the kids behave and not stress too much about what they learned. In the end, it was their fault if they couldn't do anything in the tests. I should just make sure that I have offered them the content and given homework. I couldn't agree more and it took some of the pressure off my shoulders. Another person, who helped me out a lot with the maddening and tiresome Year 9s was James. Unlike Kim, he was always there when there was a crisis in the languages corridor or when I had a situation in my form. While some colleagues tried to reduce the pressure, others applied more of it elsewhere.

PGCE all over again

As I outlined before, a Year 9 lower set French class was amongst the classes I had to teach that term. Unlike Charlotte, Emily insisted that the boys made good progress in French as the department needed as many students as possible to choose the subject as a GCSE option. This applied to German as well, however, some colleagues seemed to be more relaxed about student numbers than others. As for that class, I had the challenging task of preparing a bunch of lads, who would rather be somewhere else, for Year 10 with GCSE French or at least motivate them so that they might choose the subject. As you possibly can imagine, the class consisted of boys who either were quite weak or who could do better but didn't bother trying. The difference between a Set 4 and a Set 5 was that students in a Set 5 class were generally weak, cognitively. Most of the time they behaved badly in order to cover up their lack of general understanding. Certain students made it their mission to sabotage every lesson. Those who didn't disturb were mostly nice kids who just did their time. The class that I now had to teach was completely new to me. Emily had taught them the previous term and apparently she had a good relationship with them. So, after a month of struggling to find a connection to the boys and deliver some decent lessons to no avail, I approached Emily asking for some advice and help with that class. I wanted to know if she had any tricks that she used to make them participate or at least pay attention. She wanted to know what kind of behaviour I was dealing with and come and observe a lesson. The previous term, Claire had helped me out with difficult situations in a Year 9 class a couple of times by coming in and telling them off. I genuinely thought that the idea of observing a lesson was a suggestion with the aim to help me out. Unfortunately, things turned out to be less helpful than I could have ever imagined. I ended up regretting having asked for help. During the lesson that Emily came to observe, the boys were as quiet as they had not once been in any lesson before. Just her presence made them shut up. However, their participation left a lot to be desired. It was as if I was standing in front of a totally different bunch of students. I knew it was normal for any class to be different, usually more reserved, when another teacher was in the room. Yet I hated those students for making such a fool of me. They behaved and looked at me as if they couldn't harm a fly and as if they hadn't ever done anything wrong. I was absolutely not prepared for this, how could it have been different? I could feel the humiliation taking over my whole body. After I had described to Emily what horrible behaviour that class were displaying in French lessons, they pretended to be saints that could never wrong anybody. As I anticipated, Emily's first question in our lesson review meeting was how I had perceived the lesson and if that was the boys' usual way of conduct. As much as I tried to justify myself and explain that normally, they did not just sit there and stare at me, Emily didn't seem to be convinced. She agreed that there were some boys whose behaviour could be challenging and that the class was not a piece of cake. Nevertheless, she made it pretty clear that the problem was not the students but my teaching. What I could hear through her comments was that my teaching methods and style wasn't suitable for boys. Emily suggested that I take her lessons as a model, create my PowerPoints based on that and sent her every prepared lesson 24 hours in advance of every French class with that group. She would look at it and provide feedback so that I could make the necessary changes. Maybe Emily considered this as very useful support, but to me it felt like being treated as a trainee teacher (again) who could not be trusted to teach in her own way and manage the class. I had to conform with a way of teaching that did not reflect who I was and that I was not comfortable with. Nevertheless, I agreed with the idea, because I wasn't able to stand up for myself at that time and say that I needed a different kind of support. The level of pressure that came with this method of "supporting" me was unbearable. I always thought that support was supposed to take any kind of weight off someone's shoulders and not add more to it. But here I was, again creating lessons according to someone else's taste, trying to fulfil their ideas of a language lesson and pushing mine aside. In theory it wasn't so bad. All I had to do was following an example and twisting the activities to match the contents of my lesson. The execution however was never that straight forward. On the one hand, I couldn't identify with that teaching style, on the other hand, even a perfectly planned lesson (maybe in Emily's mind) did not make the students behave for me. Looking back, I would say that what the students needed wasn't a fancy lesson packed with games and rewards (as 99% of the time they didn't care about it), but some real consequences for their attitude and behaviour. Emily kept advising me not to be too harsh and pick my battles since the relationship between the class and I would suffer, I would end up losing them, and make my life unnecessarily harder. My question is: How can there be a relationship if there is no respect in the first place? Anyways, I wasn't in the position to oppose my acting Head of Department as she had been a teacher and at that school for a longer time. Although, I questioned many things, I couldn't say anything. I am not the bold type anyways and I felt that an environment to provide your input as a young and less experienced teacher was not given. Unlike when Claire was still there, the opinions of us younger/newer teachers hardly seemed to matter. I had the impression that unless you were really liked or matched a certain image, your views were not well received. Like that, a trainee, Emma, who had volunteered in the French department at the end of the previous term, was handled with velvet gloves and given immense importance and care just because she was likeable. She did a very good job, too, but my impression was that you had to be good at what you did and connect on a personal level in order to be awarded significance. Mentally, this took me back to my very first PGCE placement.

Initially, I was Emma's mentor. Already a few weeks into the term I had to give up that role since I was being ordered to do things that would "improve" my own teaching. Not only did I lack the time and energy to mentor a new student teacher, I probably also wasn't trusted with the job anymore. Apart from having to send in my Year 9 French lessons, I also had to attend support sessions with Beth. A performance management observation apparently had revealed that my Year 10 GCSE German lessons were not good enough either. So, what was I doing right? Not much, it seemed to me. Since Claire had praised me for my work with my previous Year 10 class, I was confident that I couldn't be doing much wrong with this one. However, during those sessions with Beth, I got the impression that almost nothing I had ever done with my Year 10 so far had been of any good. I don't remember her exact words, but what I remember is that her words made me feel discouraged and disheartened. Isn't it one thing to suggest activities to try out with a class and imposing a particular way of teaching another? I had the feeling that the latter was happening here, too, just like in Year 9. On the whole, I felt like being controlled and distrusted. They called it "coaching" but to me it was more of a "let's make her teach the right way which is our way". One evening, after the students had long gone home and I had just come back from yet another meeting with Emily, I was sitting in front of the computer trying to focus on something when Grace came into my classroom. When she asked if I was okay, I couldn't help but say no and then have an emotional breakdown after a long time. I didn't know how I was going to survive the mounting pressure and cope with the excessive workload. It was only November and I still had more than two thirds of the school term to endure. All the negative thoughts from my PGCE and NQT year re-emerged. I felt like I wasn't made for this profession and just wanted to quit everything immediately; except I couldn't. We were trying to purchase a house of our own at that time and we counted on my salary. My husband supported my thoughts of leaving my job, but I didn't want to put an end to our dream of living in our own four walls, even if it was temporarily. After my melt-down in school, I thought that talking to someone who considered my teaching good would help. I asked Claire if I could call her and get some stuff off my chest, even though she was on maternity leave. She was happy to lend me some of her time and we talked about how I was made to send in my lessons and how things had changed for me since she had gone into her time off. Claire assured me that I was a good teacher and that she had done things differently if I had asked her for help. She said that I might be too hard on myself and thriving to do everything perfectly and that the job will get easier for me. At the same time, she encouraged me to think about whether now that I knew what it could be like at the school, if this was what I wanted. On the one hand I felt relieved and on the other hand, I was still insecure. Did I really want all of this? Either way, I had to hold on to this job for now so that we could afford the house. So, as if the tremendous work pressure wasn't enough, I expected of myself that I got through this year, no matter how many and which size of stones were thrown on my way. I can't even begin to describe the state of my body and mind. I had no time for my child and the non-stop working caused me a long-term damage to my trapezius muscle. The doctor said that it was inflamed, probably due to the permanent working at the computer and bad posture. Consequently, I tried to tackle the issue ergonomically. However, over time I realised that my pain was of a different source, namely neurological. As soon as I had stressful thoughts (which was the case every minute of term time) the trapezius muscle on my right hand side would burn. During the holidays, when I didn't have to teach, send in my lessons for approval, attend countless meetings, do a disproportionate amount of admin work, waste my precious time (in which I could do even more work) in student detentions, and, not to forget, face the constantly full email inbox that contained again more tasks to complete (which also daily caused my stomach to turn already in the early morning on my way to work), I was free from any pain. The sad part is though, this pain has been coming back when having the slightest thought of having to hurry up, do multiple tasks at a time or when any worries arose; until today. Even now, there are moments when it happens, however I am able to get it under control quite quickly. I find it sad to think that this pain stems from my time at that school in London and it will always remind me of it. It reminds me of a phase of my life shaped by stress and anxiety.

Home Languages GCSE

HL, as we used to abbreviate, was at first a fun and motivating part of the French and Spanish supervisors' roles. Grace and I had the feeling that we were doing something useful for those boys who wanted to have an additional GCSE, namely in their mother tongue. It didn't require any teaching from our side as they knew their language and apart from those who didn't pick German or French GCSE, everyone else knew how the exam worked. It was just a few students who had never seen the exam format before and needed to be briefed about it. Since the students aimed for this additional certificate voluntarily, they were intrinsically motivated and only a couple of students needed to be chased and reminded to attend the short meetings during break time. Even the organisational part started out as an enjoyable aspect of my day as I got to connect with other teachers and find out about their cultures a little. The Home

Languages GCSE exams were held by internal teachers of other subjects who could speak a different language, such as Arabic or Russian, or even had it as their mother tongue. The only challenge as such was convincing them to do this and some practice with the respective students for free and putting together an exam timetable that didn't clash with their lessons. Grace and I also had to prepare the examination material for the actual tests, as well as for sending them off to the exam boards. We worked very well as a team and enjoyed the work itself. Unfortunately, this was again overshadowed by a negativity that caused all the work to be more stressful than it should have been. We needed a lot of input and guidance as to what to do along the way. Admittedly, we sometimes forgot about something or didn't consider another, but on the whole we managed to pull the Home Languages GCSEs off for the students and bottom line everything went well. It seemed to have gone unnoticed. We had to attend a few meetings in which mainly all the things we hadn't done were pointed out. We had to listen to how we had already talked about everything and that there was no time to repeat things. It was forgotten that we had never done this before and that we would have needed more guidance. Whenever we brought up HL at the end of a meeting that was scheduled for something else, I believe that we faced reluctance and were brushed off with a comment that hardly helped us. Even after the whole event, we were criticized for the things that went wrong instead of praised for the things that went right and for having managed to make this happen for the students. In my eyes, we did an ungrateful job. On the inside, I was furious. No matter how much I did or how well something went, it was neither praised nor acknowledged. The focus was on everything that was forgotten, done wrong or just happened to play out differently than planned. After the HL story, I had the feeling that there was nothing I could do to make my acting Head of Department appreciate me or at least the work I did (in her eyes, it didn't seem to be good work anyways). The HL GCSE results came back towards the end of the term, sometime in July. We didn't know that the results had come in until we asked if there was any news regarding the matter. We were not told what grades the students achieved, but again just brushed off with the information that everyone did well and passed. Maybe that's me overreacting here, but I would have expected some kind of acknowledgement at this point, at least. Who knows, maybe the Home Languages GCSE was not important to anyone, neither the job of organising it which is why it was just dumped on some inexperienced teachers to deal with it and then just forget about it. One afternoon, when I was, yet again, doing some admin and organisational work for a school trip (that I was not going to go on, but had the pleasure of making all the preparations for), the language department's line manager, Katherine, came to see me. In the first moment, I couldn't believe that she was actually expressing praise, acknowledgement and gratitude for organising and executing the Home Languages GCSEs. She said that our efforts didn't go unnoticed and that she was so happy that everything had gone well despite some hiccups. I seized this opportunity to express my disappointment about the lack of encouragement and acknowledgement during those times. For a minute, I didn't care what others thought. It had to be said. Nobody expected to make a huge deal of the whole story but a little more recognition for the job, especially as nobody else wanted to do it, would have been nice. Speaking of things that needed to be done, I have to mention the time when Grace, Katherine and I had to split Charlotte's work amongst us...

Fake Smiles

Due to health reasons, Charlotte was granted a few weeks off. During that time, her work as the Lead teacher of the subject German still had to be done, the German GCSE students prepared for their exams, and her lessons covered. Now, it's not hard to guess who was supposed to do all these things (especially as I mentioned it just a few lines before). The German department, consisting of us three remaining German teachers, was under pressure, more than it already had been. An unspeakable amount of work had to be done in Charlotte's absence. Especially the lesson planning for her GCSE classes and the creation of resources for the after-school support sessions for those GCSE students as well as supervising them was extremely time consuming. This was probably the reason for calling in a meeting in which Grace and I (in separate meetings) were told that, excuse my language, shit was going to hit the fan. Katherine led the meetings in the presence of Emily. Funnily enough, now that a buck load of work on top of everything else was going to be dumped on us, it seemed as if Emily was as empathetic and friendly as no one could be. She hadn't been this nice to me since I had taken over a Year 8 class the previous term after Sylvie, a trainee teacher had given up, or rather was made to quit, teaching them. Unfortunately, Sylvie didn't seem to be able to deliver her lessons as planned despite the many hours that Emily or I sat down with her to talk things through and many times she did the opposite of what had been agreed upon. This could be frustrating and I could understand that one might lose patience with Sylvie. At one point, it became clear that Sylvie couldn't stay. She was taken out of our school and placed in another one in order to complete her training. Now, Emily and I had to teach the classes that had been given to Sylvie. Emily was very happy when I took over the class and treated me as a saviour, because I had the class under control and made progress with them after they had been having rather chaotic and fruitless lessons with Sylvie. However, the exact same class that behaved badly for Sylvie and well for me in Year 8 decided to be less responsive towards me in the new term, although I had built a good relationship with them and simultaneously, the exact same Emily behaved differently towards me in this term. There seemed to be a pattern and it was hard for me to accept that when something was needed from me, I was treated like a hero and when things didn't go too well I felt I was being treated like the rank and file.

My relationship with Emily had changed ever since she had come into my lesson with the difficult French class. We stopped talking about private stuff like we used to. I felt like she didn't want to connect on a personal level with me anymore, in fact, she only spoke to me if she had to. At first, I was really sad, because I had lost what could have become a friendship. Then, I thought to myself that there was no point in dwelling on this and make my life even harder than it already was at that point.

If there was one thing I couldn't stand, it was the marking of student books. Since the beginning of my teaching career in England, marking books had been the part of the job I probably hated the most. They either had to be carried home and most of the time it was a bunch of more than thirty, or I had to stay in school (even) longer in order to flip through them. This school had a very strict marking policy and if I had stuck to it, I probably would have ended up sleeping in school. So, I came up with my own policy and tried to ensure to have marked every class's books once a half-term, unsuccessfully. I just didn't want to agree that this was the only way to give students immediate feedback on their learning and progress. I had never heard of book-marking in my years as a student. The only reason teachers would ever collect our books was to see if we were treating it well and to give someone a reward for treating it extremely well. Obviously, they checked if we were completing the tasks that were set during a lesson but how on earth is one supposed to keep checking that every task was completed correctly by every student?! Call me stupid, but how is every student in a class going to get every answer or most of the answers right at all times? Isn't learning an individual process where every child is supposed to have their very own strengths and weaknesses? Then why were we desperately trying to make every student be on the same level of knowledge? I will elaborate on the answer in a later section, but now back to the book-marking which cost me a good lesson rating just before I left the school. Yes, I had to find yet another work place as we had completed on a house in West Sussex, in April. There was only one school in the surroundings of the town we were going to move to which was looking for a foreign languages teacher. A lot was on stake, I had to get this job. Although, I was playing with thoughts about quitting teaching again, I needed to land this teaching post so that we would be able to pay our mortgage. So, again I was loaded with pressure. Sometimes, I still wonder how I was successful at the first shot with so much depending on it. The interview committee offered me the post and I accepted without hesitation. Now, almost everything was set for our new life outside of London. We found a house and I secured a job. Or son got a place in a nursery not too far from the house and my work place. The only point left on the agenda was finding a job for my husband, which presented itself to be more difficult than expected. Luckily, this problem got solved when a family acquaintance decided to take on a second fuel station after he had heard that we were moving into that area. He gave my husband the responsibility of running and managing the place. Anyways, back to London. Every permanent member of staff at the school had to undergo a lesson observation once a term in order to prove their ability to teach good lessons. It was the school's way of securing good quality of teaching and learning. From my point of view, it was just another way of controlling and micro-managing teachers and exercising pressure on them. I had already done my performance management observation, but as there were a couple of things that were not to the observer's liking, I had to do a follow-up one. The person doing the observations was another teacher designated for this task. Towards the end of the year, she became too busy to come to my follow-up observation herself so that she asked Katherine to do it. I didn't understand why I had to go through this, now that I was going to leave for good anyway. I asked if it was really necessary as so many things were going on, but I was told that it was school policy and that I shouldn't worry too much about it. The perfectionist that I was, the days leading up to the observation, I spent hours after work preparing a solid lesson that would leave Katherine without any points to criticise. How naïve I was, again. I should have known better. No matter how hard you tried and even if it was a perfect lesson, the observer would always find something for you to improve. Even if the observer personally had nothing to say, the form that he or she had to fill in and the people looking at it would expect something written in the box "areas for improvement" or "opportunities for improvement". Surely, there would always be something to be commented on. Everybody is different and (normally) teaches differently. What works for me doesn't necessarily work for someone else. In my eyes, teaching is very personal and kind of an art that cannot and should not be controlled by others. Yes, one could learn from one another and take advice and tips into consideration but at the end of the day, one has to figure out for oneself what works and what doesn't. Unfortunately, what many schools in England seem to do is standardising teaching. Complete nonsense to me. I also couldn't understand how one lesson was supposed to determine whether your teaching was "outstanding", "good", "required improvement", or "inadequate". These were the ratings used by Ofsted to grade schools and my school used them to grade teachers. A few young colleagues were as irritated by these ratings as I was. Apparently, teachers weren't supposed to be graded anymore according to Ofsted. Yet, our school kept doing it as it "helped" everyone being on top of their teaching. Ofsted apparently also said that book-marking shouldn't be considered in lesson evaluations anymore. I keep saying "apparently" because frankly, I never really familiarised myself with Ofsted requirements. I found it difficult and annoying enough to be meeting certain department requirements, so I treated myself not to stress about Ofsted too much. During my teaching career in England, I was also lucky enough not having to undergo an Ofsted inspection at any school. So, the day of the observation was around the corner and I just about remembered to mark the class's books the day before. I had only marked them once before that, so I made an effort to write extra comments and put extra ticks and smileys in between the two dates of marking so it somewhat looked like I had looked at them more than twice. It was such a tedious job. As you now know, I hated marking and it was a waste of my precious time. But I managed to do it and I was quite sure that this time, the observation would go well. Katherine came into my Year 7 German class. I loved teaching them as they were still curious, engaged, and reverent. The majority of the class was bright and produced good work as a rule. Consequently, I was confident that everything would go well, unless all the kids decided to be someone else on that day (like the Year 9 French class when Emily came in). This was not likely to happen in a class of Year 7, so I was positive. You can probably already guess, how this is going to end. Like almost each time I had a good feeling about something, this time, too, I was disappointed. As I had hoped, there was nothing to criticise about the lesson itself. Katherine said that she was impressed by how much the boys had learnt already and how engaged they were throughout the lesson. She praised me for managing the class effectively and for making them do the right amount of work while challenging the stronger students. What else would one want from a lesson? And yet, there was something that bothered Katherine so much that she couldn't even give me a "good" for my lesson but left me with a "requires improvement", even though I only had a couple of weeks left at that school. The reason for this rating was that I hadn't marked the books frequently enough and therefore the boys didn't have enough feedback on their learning. Let this sink in for a moment... So, my lesson was brilliant but only deserved the rating "requires improvement" because I didn't waste enough time flipping through student books. Great. I asked her if this rating was going to affect my new post and she said no, that it was just for their records. So, what was the point of putting me through this? Was it to watch me being more stressed than I already had been? Was it to simply waste my time? Was it some kind of revenge for something that I didn't know I had done? Was it an attempt to show me that I didn't fit in anyway and that it was good that I was leaving? Emily even once said to me in one of our meetings that this might not be the right school for me and that for some people it takes time to find a place where they really belong. But why treat someone like this if they had already handed in their notice? I really do not know. And any colleague outside my department that I spoke to about this as well as Grace didn't understand it either. Why make a member of staff who had already resigned go through a performance management observation and then give them a rating that didn't reflect the quality of the observed lesson? Maybe you see the logic behind this. Fact is, I don't, never did, never will. As I said before, I don't believe that marking books is going to change a student's progress significantly. Even if it did, I believe that the observer is supposed to rate what he or she OBSERVED during the LESSON, which is why it's called a LESSON OBSERVATION, and not rate other aspects that didn't happen in the observed lesson itself. And even if the book marking had to be considered in the rating, why couldn't it just have been a point in "opportunities for improvement" and not be the reason for my teaching to "require improvement"? You can see that it really bothered me. On the one hand, I was upset about this unfairness coming from Katherine who had been so supportive and all the time, on the other hand, I couldn't believe that I was being sent off like this after all the work I did for the department. Maybe they tried to teach me a lesson; the lesson being that marking books is probably THE most important part of teaching... Unfortunately for them, that wasn't what I took from this whole story. I believed, and I still believe, that someone just wanted to punch me in the face and make me feel awful before I went on to another school. The last day of school was most certainly another punch in the face. Although, I was longing for this day to arrive for months, on the morning of the last day of term, I was upset. This was going to be the last time that I'd walk into that school building, drop my stuff in my classroom, go over to Grace to say good morning and have a chat with her. I really liked working with her and we made a great team. We both had a difficult time managing our workload that year and we were there for each other. We always had each other's backs and a shoulder to cry on during meltdowns. All this had come to an end and I somehow felt sorry for leaving her alone. It was really difficult saying good-bye to Grace, but I knew that it wouldn't be forever. We had become good friends. It was much easier to say farewell to the rest of the department. Usually, the Head of Department wrote the farewell speeches with help of another colleague. When Katherine read mine, it became clear very quickly that Emily had nothing to do with it. I'm going to go out on a limb and say maybe she didn't want to because she didn't have anything nice to say about me. During my farewell speech, she didn't even seem to listen properly. In my eyes, she just sat there indifferently and was chatting to some colleague next to her. And when everyone clapped, she didn't bother to do the same. Maybe it's childish of me and weird that I noticed all these little things and maybe I made it up in my head, but the last part of the day confirmed the vibes I was having during the speeches. The languages department met in Emily's room after the staff gathering. It was a little tradition to meet once before everyone went into their holidays. The previous term, when Claire was still Head of Department, we had a good vibe. We all sat down, talked for a little bit, handed over the gift to Dave the trainee, received little thank you gifts from him, hugged each other and parted ways. This time, it was just awkward. Everyone just stood there, not knowing what to do. There was no atmosphere that invited anyone to get comfortable. I was sitting down but couldn't wait to leave. When everyone was there, Emily picked up a gift bag from behind her desk, put it down in front of me without any kind of prelude and just said: "Right, here you go." There was no eye contact, no smile, and no warmth in this gesture. I felt like saying "No, thank you, I don't want to receive a gift in this manner" but as usual I kept my mouth shut, feeling hurt about the indifference that was being displayed towards me. What's a gift when the person handing it over can't even make eye contact with you or can't even slap on a smile for the sake of it? So many smiles were faked in the past months, but when it actually counted and would have made things a little nicer and less awkward, the aversion was obvious. Despite everything, after packing up all my stuff I went to each colleague in my department to say good-bye, even to Emily. Despite everything, I was not going to stoop down to the same level of rudeness. However, what I was going to do was leaving everything behind and not look back. I remember thinking "Oh no, never again" when Beth said "All the best, keep in touch and let us know how things are". I knew instantly that I was not going to keep in touch with anyone but Grace. I just faked a smile, said "Sure!" and left. That day was the last time that I ever saw or heard from anyone in that department, apart from Grace.

10. One last time

First Impressions Deceive

With a huge sense of relief that I was done with the school in London, I spent the summer holidays preparing for our move to the new house and our trip to the motherland for my brother-in-law's wedding. Thus, there was hardly any time to prepare for school, my new school in West Sussex. This time, I wasn't very concerned about my lack of preparation, though. In the getting-to-know-the-department meetings, I got the vibe that I was well-prepared already and since this was going to be my third school now, I had gathered some resources I could recycle for my new classes. Also, I had filled up my hard drive with as many resources as possible from the shared drive before the holidays. So, I had material to fall back on. What I liked best about my new MFL (modern foreign languages) colleagues was that they seemed to share my views on marking books. The fact that they didn't have a strict marking policy in the department was excellent news for me. I got the impression that this school didn't make the language department do stuff that the teachers didn't consider useful or necessary. I was convinced that this was going to be the school where I would be staying for a long time, despite the many issues around safeguarding. There was a long session regarding this at the school on the introduction day for new staff just before the holidays. I was disappointed to realise that I had landed in a rather underprivileged area of England where problems with for instance drugs, child neglect, mental health problems, and so on, were on the daily agenda of the school's safeguarding officers. We teachers had to look out for any signs or suspicious behaviour in the children which I thought was a huge responsibility. Of course, as a teacher one has the duty to make sure that one's students are keeping well and to notice and communicate any abnormalities. However, this school made it sound as if something was definitely going to happen in one of our classes at some point and we had to be ready for it. After the induction day, I went home with a strange feeling. Was this the type of school I wanted to work in? I pushed that question aside quickly, as, whether I liked the place or not, I had no choice. We had a mortgage to pay. Also, it seemed as if I was going to have more freedom in my teaching and the way I worked. “You can’t have everything” I thought to myself and remained positive, looking forward to starting a new life in our new town, in our new home with new jobs.

My first impression of my classes was quite positive. The kids seemed nice and open for the new French and German teacher. They were interested in me as a person and showed willingness to participate and learn. Apparently my predecessor was a little older and not very popular with the children, so that they were grateful for someone younger with more energy. Yet, it didn’t take very long for me to realise that this first impression was misleading. Now, that sounds a little harsh. Let’s take a closer look at why the students and the school were not what I had thought they would be. Generally speaking, a polite and respectful student was a rare occurrence. The majority of children were either indifferent, rude or simply disrespectful towards teachers. On break duty for instance, I had to deal with smoking students from Year 9 to Year 11, standing in one corner of the playground, visible for everyone, and not putting the cigarette out when asked to but blowing the smoke in my face or simply ignoring my presence. During lessons, I had to battle with some boys who were ditching their own class and actively disturbing mine from outside the window. As if the disrespect from students I didn't know wasn't enough, I also had to face sheer rudeness coming from my own students. To name but a few, there were Brad, Lucas, Esther, and Lucy.

Restorative (In)Justice

In my 23 years of living in Germany and in my two previous schools where I had taught, I hadn't experienced any type of racism (maybe I was just lucky). I accepted that some Year 11 students felt the need to tell me how to spell English words or where to place commas, and subtly communicated that I wouldn't know because I am not English. But when Brad, a Year 9 student, aped me with an Indian accent after I had demanded several times that he stop talking to his neighbour and distracting him, I couldn't believe what I saw and heard. He sat there, right in front of me, repeating my words, mimicking an Indian accent. For me this meant that he had assumed by my looks that I was Indian and that he took out the right to attack me on these grounds. Now, you could argue that I shouldn't have taken it personally, as I don't talk the way he portrayed it anyway, but in my eyes, he knew exactly why he had chosen that particular accent in which he repeated my demand to be quiet. That lesson was the last lesson he attended with me in German as he had several issues and needed more and different attention so that he was put into the part of the school for difficult students. It was a different building which I hadn't even known that it existed up to that point. The fact that the school ran such a "section" for students who were hard to get through to, speaks for itself. This is of course, again, generally speaking. In every school, there would always be the small exceptional minority that stands out for the opposite behaviour. However, in this school, the friendly students, siding with their teacher, had a tough draw. One day, a student whom I didn't know swore at me for demanding that he and his friends stop fooling around in front of my classroom at the end of break. When asking for his name, nobody wanted to tell me, except Owen. He was not scared to expose the boy who told me to f*** off. Clearly, the other kids of that class were shocked that Owen gave me the name just like that. They were right to be scared. Somehow, the boy who swore found out that Owen had exposed him to me, waited around for Owen when he was on his way home from school, and punched him in the face so that his jaw dislocated. Owen didn't come to school for a few days and at first I thought that he was just ill until I asked the class if they knew anything about Owen. They looked at each other and asked me if I didn't know what had happened. When I heard this terrible story, I felt so guilty and furious at the same time. What was going on with those kids? Apparently, this matter was already being dealt with by the parents, they had even involved the police. I just had a hard time accepting that it was caused by me wanting to know that aggressive boy's name. Everyone else, however, didn't seem to associate me with the incident at all. I was relieved and frustrated at the same time; frustrated that there was nothing that I could do about the happenings, relieved that I wasn't to be blamed. When I apologised to Owen for causing this to him, he said that it wasn't my fault and that it was his decision to expose that boy. I couldn't believe that a good child had to suffer injuries although he had done nothing wrong. What a place... One can only hope that it has become better over the last few years. Despite the racist behaviour, Brad was at least not violent and not as annoying as Lucas from the same year group. Brad had a very poor attendance quote from the beginning on and when he was there, the worst he did was talking to his neighbours; apart from the other incident, of course. Lucas on the other hand, seemed to have made it his mission to sabotage every single lesson. He actively sought opportunities to interrupt me, disrupt my lesson and distract the whole class. When I addressed his behaviour, there was no winning with him. Basically, he was my new Oliver, just in a different school. What more is there to say? I dreaded every lesson with that class, although most of the other kids were nice and willing to learn, just like in Oliver's class. What made the lessons even more intense for me was the fact that a student from the "other" building joined the class after a few weeks into the term. He was said to be one of the most difficult ones who at first was only allowed into lessons with his supporter. This alone made me extremely nervous inside. What was I about to go through? He seemed quite popular with the other students, especially the girls. In the end, I never had a real problem with that boy and I was deemed lucky for that by my colleagues. Not only the boys gave me a hard time, but there were troublemakers amongst the girls, too. There was Esther who just exuded negativity. You just needed to look at her face to guess that she hated going to school and that she was totally indifferent towards education, let alone her teachers. In her French class, she started off being rather discreet. She would occasionally chat with her neighbour Rowan, who was, in general, more disruptive. Yet, every time I asked her to stop chatting or to concentrate on the lesson, there was this look on her face... She never looked at me directly, on purpose. All I got was a gum-chewing mug with an expression that showed me how much I had disturbed her little conversation with her neighbour or some other friend behind her. One day, the chatting in class was excessive and I had warned everyone that if there was any word uttered out of order, I'd send that person to the so-called silent room. The silent room was a place for students who couldn't behave in class. They were sent there so that lessons could carry on normally and the troublemakers could do some silent work by themselves. I will elaborate further on this room in just a few moments. Despite my warning, Esther thought she had to chat to her neighbour again. In order to make my point clear and to be consistent in my behaviour management strategy, I asked her to leave the class and go to the silent room. That was the first time, Esther actually looked at me and acknowledged my existence. Sadly, what followed her scornful look was something that expressed her wish for my absence. She started off trying to justify her talking. Apparently, my lessons were so boring and she wasn't learning anything. I replied that if she listened more instead of chatting to her neighbour Rowan so much, she'd actually learn something and realise that we were doing fun stuff, too. I thought that I had won that battle, but then Esther unpacked some more of her wisdom and said that I was such a bad teacher and that I should be sacked. After that, she made her way out of the classroom. I soldiered through the rest of the lesson, trying to pretend that what Esther had said didn't bother me at all. Except it did. In my break duty after that lesson, some familiar thoughts were flashing across my mind. Did I want to be here? Did I want to be spoken to like this? Did I want to do this day after day for the rest of my life? Did I work so hard for being treated like this? Of course, I was dealing with children, who most of the time didn't know what they were talking about and whose aim was often to just push their teachers' buttons just because it's fun. Nevertheless, I knew that the answer to all those questions was "No". I didn't have enough time to think my thoughts through as break was over and I had to dive right into the next lesson. I remember hoping that the kids would be nice as I couldn't take another child being rude to my face. Another reason was that the more children I sent to the silent room, the more parent emails I'd have to write and the more so-called restorative conversations I'd have to hold. As soon as a student was sent to the silent room, the parents were notified via text message. The silent room was not just a room were students where students were sent, but it was a room supervised by teachers who tried their best to make the students do some silent work during their time there. Most of the time the kids just sat there doing nothing at all or even carrying on with their bad behaviour. Once I sent a Year 7 girl to the silent room. Afterwards, I was threatened by the mother that if I ever sent her poor daughter (who didn't make any impression of being afraid of anything or anyone but constantly talked back or pulled a face when being reprimanded) to the silent room again where the little girl didn't know anybody, she'd take action. Unfortunately for her, I had the Head of Year on my side and fortunately for me, I didn't have to go through a restorative conversation with that little brat as clearly, both, mother and daughter were in the wrong. Now what is a restorative conversation? It was meant to be a talk between the student and the teacher who sent him or her to the silent room in order to restore their relationship. As a teacher you'd hope that the student would come to their senses and apologise for their inacceptable and oftentimes inappropriate behaviour. Sadly, that was seldom the case. It was more the teachers who had to suck up to the students in order to "restore the relationship", which basically meant that there was a clean slate in that moment. In most cases though, the same kid would just do the same things in the next lesson with the same teacher. Something clearly went wrong in that silent room system. For many children it was actually a retreat from their lessons. On top of that, they were being flattered (I'm exaggerating here) by their teachers. What more of an entertainment could there be for a teenager who can't be bothered about education? The only thing that was a disturbing factor was the fact that a message went out to the parents, but even that wasn't much of a threat to many pupils. I had to face a very uncomfortable situation with a girl whom I had sent to the silent room. I don't recall the exact words that were spoken, but I do remember the way I felt during and after the talk. My feelings ranged from pure, blood-boiling rage to humiliation and wanting to cry then and there. The girl, Lucy, had relentlessly disturbed my lesson (as she usually did, but more subtly and she had always gotten away with it) by chatting non-stop and making inappropriate and offensive comments towards me. I thought that sending her away for once would teach her a lesson and make her realise that her behaviour was not acceptable. I was too naïve to see that she probably knew that and that she was doing the things she did very consciously and purposefully. When I tried to confront her, she didn't give me a chance to finish a single sentence. Lucy behaved as though she was not in the wrong at all and that I was the one who had treated her badly during the lesson. She was being exceptionally rude and a blatant liar. The way she looked at me was as if I didn't even have the right to exist, let alone stand in front of her and speak to her. Yes, she was only a child, less than half my age, but those who have been in such kind of situations will understand how difficult it is to keep your cool and not lose it right in front of such a vicious kid. I say vicious as Lucy not only liked to disturb lessons and go against her teachers, she also thrived in emotionally abusing other children during a lesson. She was the kind of child where you didn't know whether to feel sorry for or be afraid of. Lucy must have seen my eyes filling up with tears as she didn't back off one bit. The fact that I let her see my emotions gave her confidence and in the end I just said "I can't do this", turned around as the tears started to crawl and headed to my classroom where I sat and cried while Lucy was probably celebrating her victory. While I was trying to recover from what had just happened I noticed something. I wanted to become a teacher because I liked children and I loved working with them, passing on my knowledge and passion for languages to them. Working in this system, especially at this school, made me starting to hate children. I noticed that in the past few years, there had been too many incidents for my taste to believe that children must be loved, no matter what and that deserved our affection and respect regardless of their behaviour. I just couldn't believe this anymore. Too much had happened. I was afraid of ending up hating all children and I knew that I had to stop before it was too late.

Tipping point

The love for the work with young people and the fact that I had my freedom in how I taught my subjects had kept me going all this time. Sadly, both these factors started to cease. Due to all the happenings with students, and I have only listed a few of many more in this book, I started to lose my passion for languages and for what I thought was my calling: being a teacher. The latter happened when senior management came up with the idea of implementing strategies to standardise the teaching at the school. Up until October half-term I thought I had the freedom of teaching however it suited me and my personality, as well as the class. This was put an end to by introducing some principles established by an expert of educational psychology. Basically these principles outline how to best deliver your lessons. Don't get me wrong, the principles are great and make total sense. The disturbing part was that those principles seemed to have become a dogma at the school and the teachers were checked up on whether they were implementing them in their lessons. The heads of department were meant to do so-called learning walks within their subject to ensure that their colleagues were explicitly structuring their lessons based on these ideas. If a principle was not implemented, it was noted down and brought up in a conversation after the learning walk. I hated that I was forced to explicitly name my lesson segments according to those principles and that I had to implement them in a certain order. I want to stress again that I am not going against these concepts, but the way this was imposed upon us, was, in my eyes, not the right one. Every good teacher knows that those theories are part of effective and student-friendly teaching, yet teaching is, I believe, not something that can be standardised, let alone be stipulated how to do! Teaching is an art and every artist is different. Everyone has their own personality with methods and ways of teaching that might work for them but not for the colleague. Yes, there are certain factors that enhance student learning and progress, but is everything about progress and results? It seems the answer for English schools is 'yes'. I will talk about this aspect in the chapter *Priceless Information* in the section *The System*. Now back to my internal struggle and the tipping point, which occurred at an INSET day after the Christmas holidays. Already before the holidays, I was on a low point, seeing myself putting an end to my teaching career. I was browsing on the Internet looking for other opportunities with my languages and other skills that I had acquired as a teacher over the years. I even randomly and aimlessly applied for a few positions in corporate companies. I didn't think that I'd have any chance of finding another field of work as quickly as I had liked to. So, when I was sitting in a presentation, held by the head of teaching and learning (yes, such a position exists) of another school, I finally decided to quit putting up with all this nonsense. He was actually telling us, that a student's intelligence can be measured and that a student's progress can be predicted based on results achieved at the end of primary school. At least this is what I understood and upon double-checking with colleagues, I understood right. In the presentation, there was a graph and a chart and all sorts of visualisations to convey the above message. Students were treated as an object of business and teaching was seen as an act of doing business. Although my heart ached in that moment, my head had decided: I was done teaching. Forever. I did not sign up for this and I was not going to do it any longer. It was over. Luckily, for my mind not to short-circuit after this decision, I was going to have an interview with a renowned company after the INSET day.

11. Detour

Poker game

Now that I had finally made up my mind about leaving this school, I somehow had to break it to my colleagues and the senior leadership without risking having to stop working immediately. Call me a coward, but I wanted to be diplomatic. I didn't have the strength to say that the reason for my leaving was the unpleasant students at that school and the impractical school system. Instead, I threw myself under the bus saying that I couldn't keep up with the work while being a mum. I claimed that I wasn't able to do justice to neither my profession nor to my family. Everyone understood my reasons and I felt ten pounds lighter having "opened up". I was even offered help with planning lessons and marking exams, though I felt bad making my colleagues work more, which is why I did all my work until the end. I didn't shout it from the rooftops that I had already had a couple of interviews, because I wanted to keep everything as open as possible. I needed to ensure a smooth transition between jobs so that we wouldn't fall short in terms of finances. It was a poker game. When I was asked when about I was going to hand in my notice and until when I'd keep working, I just said that I'd have to figure things out and that I'd tell them as soon as possible. In the meantime, I was putting everything on one card: a credit card company. My plan was to land that job which I interviewed remotely for on the day of the INSET. The day after the meeting with that company I had a meeting with a car parts company, but I was really hoping to get into a well-known establishment. My hope was that my thirtieth birthday would be my lucky day as I was supposed to receive the outcome of the interview then. According to a good friend of mine, I had done well in the interview. She works in the finance sector and upon my telling about the interview, she said that provided I was replaying the interview exactly as it went I had the job. The position I had applied for during the Christmas holidays was as a credit controller, which meant that I had to ensure that private card holders adhered to their payment schedules. The interview was mostly set up as any other I had gone through before, except this time I had to take part in a role-play. A long-term client hadn't made his payment on time so that his credit card had been blocked by the company. My task was to work around the irritation this had caused him and figure out a way to initiate a win-win situation. Apparently, I had done this to great satisfaction of the team leaders who conducted my interview as I received a call from the recruiter with positive news on my birthday. She said that the team leaders were extremely impressed with my communication skills and my overall performance in the interview and that it was clear that amongst all applicants I would get the job. As you can imagine I was beyond happy about the outcome and it gave us one more reason to celebrate that night. There was only this one little catch: it was compulsory to work on two Saturdays a month. I assured the recruiter that I was totally willing to do this but that it was kind of impossible with a child and a husband with a fixed work schedule, upon which she said that it shouldn't be a problem to work around the Saturdays and that she would get back to me regarding this the following week. I didn't think much about it and was sure that having a child would work in my favour here. So, on the following Monday, I was all prepared to be delivered the fantastic news that it was no issue at all that I couldn't work on Saturdays and that I still had the job (I'm sure you know by now that I used to be quite naïve). But there was no call, neither on Tuesday. Now, I was nervous. Why wasn't the recruiter calling me? Was that it? Did I blow it? This was so nerve wracking. If it had been up to me, I would have emailed the recruiter on Monday evening already. However, my finance friend advised me to wait 48 hours before making a move. If I still hadn't heard anything on Wednesday, I could get in touch.

So, I waited, as I was told to. It was one of the hardest waits for me that I can remember. Then, finally, on Wednesday afternoon I got the call. I would like to tell my old self that "of course it is going to be a problem if you can't fulfil a requirement of the position", but I guess I had to go through all these experiences in order to lose my naivety. The recruiter phoned me to say that it didn't work out with the credit controller position because of the fact that I couldn't work on Saturdays. However, she took so long to call me back as she was sorting out another opportunity for me. A different department in the same company was looking for a new addition to their team. The good part was that they didn't work on Saturdays and that they dealt with corporate instead of private clients. The only catch was that I had to attend yet another interview. Of course, I agreed to it. I wouldn't let any chance to get out of that school slip my fingers. I was happy to have gotten another opportunity, but I dreaded another long wait for the decision. Just this time, I didn't have to wait long, at all. The interview seemed to be just a formality. The team leader was made aware of my interview performance for the other team and so she only asked me some superficial questions. At the end, she promised me the job straight away. This was almost too easy now... What a roller-coaster ride! I couldn't believe what just had happened. I had a job at a great company and I could quit teaching now.

In between two worlds

My new team leader at the new company agreed that I could start just after Easter as the school wouldn't let me go before the spring term had ended. So, I handed in my notice for the last day of school before the Easter holidays. On the one hand, I was looking forward to beginning a new career in a couple of months, on the other hand, I dreaded those couple of months in school. Especially, because my language colleagues, namely my head of department and the second in charge, decided to reallocate some students to different sets. For me it meant that I had more troublemakers in my classes and the Year 10 German class that I had taught was reallocated. This course of action was couched in diplomatic terms. It was said that by giving up the important classes and the better students, there would be less pressure and work for me. I tried to think that they meant well, but I couldn't shake the feeling that these measures were only taken to ensure that I didn't neglect my classes since I had an expiry date at the school. It was weird not being included in any department conversations anymore and in retrospect I wonder if, despite them saying that they understood where I was coming from, my colleagues were actually upset or even annoyed. And I can understand if they were as apparently there had been a history of teachers leaving mid-term. To be frank, I couldn't care less about what was going on in school. Yes, I had to deal with more of the annoying students, but I didn't have to put my heart and soul into my lessons anymore and I was more worried about the general circumstances than how my colleagues treated me. While I was counting down my weeks and days, Covid 19 was making its way from China to Europe. The news from Spain and Italy scared everyone, or let's say most, at school and the "Corona virus" was the only important topic for students. In every lesson, the question whether the school was going to close and if there was going to be a lockdown in the UK as well popped up. Of course, nobody knew and the teachers didn't have an answer to that. Secretly, I was hoping that the school would just close out of precaution. That way, I wouldn't have to drag myself to work for the next few weeks until I started my new job. But school didn't close for the next three weeks or so. Less and less students came to school and eventually more and more teachers stayed home due to having Covid 19 symptoms, what used to be just a cold. One morning, my son started coughing and had a runny nose. When I called nursery and asked what to do about it, they asked me to keep him home. Within the last few days, the measurements to keep the virus from spreading became very strict. As soon as you or a family member had any cold symptom, maintaining distance was called for. So, my son couldn't go to nursery which meant that I couldn't go to work. Two days later, I fell sick myself and the week after, the school was closed. The UK was in lockdown. As much as I was wishing my time at the school away, the fact that my teaching career ended abruptly like this made me feel a little heartbroken. I had no chance to say goodbye to my students, at least the ones who cared, and to my colleagues. It felt like I was being pulled out of a movie without being given the time to see what happens in the end. In addition, I didn't know what was happening with my new job. I hadn't heard from Rose, my team leader, in a while and I became a little nervous, wondering whether I could still on-board despite the pandemic and the lockdown. Worried about my situation, I emailed Rose asking if everything was still going to happen the way it had been agreed. It was such a relief when she scheduled a video call to assure me that everything was fine and that literally everyone at the company had been busy sorting out the new working-from-home model. The existing staff was provided with equipment in order to be able to complete their work at home and the on-boarding of new team members was not a priority at that time. In fact, I was lucky. The recruitment of new staff was paused due to the pandemic after I had been hired. I was told to just hang in there and wait for further emails while school told me not to worry about providing any work for students to do at home. I was kind of in two places at once, but had nothing to do. When my new equipment from the head office arrived via courier, I was relieved. Eventually, it was the end of March and my official last day of work at school. Rose had communicated that my start at the company would be delayed by a couple of weeks, so I had so much free time and I wasn't used it. There were so many things I had always wanted to do around the house, with my son or for myself but I just didn't feel like it. As a family, we used the time to get our garden done. When we bought the house we had to decide between having the solicitor fees payed or the garden done. The choice wasn't difficult. We took advantage of the fact that I was double-paid in April. I received my last salary from school and my first salary from my new company so that we could afford doing the garden. I can only say that those were strange times and I'm sure, I speak for everyone.

Welcome, how can I help?

This was a phrase that I had been using a lot in my new job. As strange and as difficult as the times were for many people during the pandemic, I can't help but feel and say that the regulations to contain the Covid 19 virus did something good. My stress level was reduced not only by the fact that I only had to work 9 – 5 and not worry about work after my shift finished, but especially by the work-from-home system. I didn't have to drive back and forth, be stuck in traffic and spend a ridiculous amount of money on fuel. Furthermore, I didn't have to get up early and I could have lunch at home and be there for my son while working. The latter was more demanding than I had anticipated, but I was happy that I finally got to just be with my son. Before I started, I had been worried that I'd be unchallenged in my new job. I was convinced otherwise, quickly. There was a lot to learn about processes and systems and I loved being the student for a change. I had always wondered what I'd do with a notebook that is thick with hundreds of pages. When training for my new position, I recognised how useful such a notebook could be. I had filled almost a whole diary with notes about information on numerous systems and platforms, as well as processes on how to work a client request. According to my trainer and Rose, I completed my training and passed all tests with flying colours so that I was put on the phone line quite soon. After some initial stage fright, I got the hang of how to provide good customer service. Now, I only had to work the systems correctly, follow the right processes and take care of the clients in a professional and gratifying manner, all at the same time. After the first ten phone calls, I got used to all of it, too and started enjoying my new job. The best part of my day was catching up with my team in the daily virtual huddles in the morning and chatting to a couple of my closer colleagues towards the end of our shift. For the first time, I was actually happy at work. Compared to what I was doing before this was a walk in the park. I got up as late as possible as I didn't have to rush to the office. Instead, I often had breakfast in front of my laptop and wore PJ bottoms. This is obviously not a ground-breaking piece of information after having gone through a pandemic, but at that time, it was all new to me and I suppose to almost everyone. At 5 pm, I switched off my laptop and also any thoughts about work. Again, this was something new for me as I used to think about work 24/7. "What a life!" I thought. The only down-side to this new situation was the salary. We had to accept that I earned a thousand Pounds less than before. Thanks to Covid 19, I didn't have to drive to work and spend a significant amount of money on fuel. And since I was working from home anyway, our son didn't have to attend nursery full-time. Again, some money saved. I'd like to believe that if it hadn't been for the Corona virus and me working from home, we wouldn't have made ends meet with such a huge cut in our household income. When I left teaching, I didn't care about how much money I was going to make in my new job. I just needed to be elsewhere and money was not of prime importance to me. So, all in all, things were going well. I was so quick to pick up my new role that I was appointed the new-hire trainer of the team. For me that was great as I was now teaching again. When the new team members did well, it reflected well on me, if they didn't do a good job, I was not held responsible. This was just great. Soon, I was even invited to explain certain aspects or a whole system to the new batch of new-hires, who were on-boarded once the company got used to the situation, during their training. I was quite optimistic that I had a chance of moving up the company ladder sooner than later. My aim was to become an actual new-hire trainer. I would have flexible working hours, I would be creating teaching material and teaching new-hires, and I would be earning more. Looking back, I think that my heart had already known what my head was not yet ready to admit: the job was fun and it was definitely less stressful than a teaching career, but something was missing. Now I know that at that time I was happy, but didn't have a sense of accomplishment. Nevertheless, I was very ambitious and did everything that was needed in order to reach my goal and I was sure to be on the right track.

Spoke in a wheel

While I was working so enthusiastically towards my goal, we had other plans, privately. After I had finally made peace with the fact that my first delivery was so traumatic, I was mentally ready to be pregnant again. We were excited to grow our family and what better time could we have chosen to try for another baby? I was working from home, I was not stressed, we had a spacious enough house... What more did we need? The answer is modesty. Unlike during my first pregnancy, I wanted to be more positive and less nervous this time, when it happened. I decided to think myself into happiness the "Secret"-style. When I fell pregnant in December, I thought I knew that nothing could happen to me and started to plan for the new family member.

Between me and my husband, especially I was over confident. We were both excited to welcome our new offspring, though. I had only told a couple of close colleagues at work that I was pregnant and celebrated the fact that I was working from home. The tiredness and nausea would have been difficult to handle otherwise. On my birthday, we told our families about the news. Even then I thought that nothing could ever destroy this dream, burst my bubble, because telling everyone on my birthday would bring me luck. Yet, the dream turned into a nightmare only a month later. I started bleeding. The nurses on the maternity ward assured me that this was normal at this stage and that I shouldn't be worried, unless the bleeding increased. And it did. We went to A&E on a Saturday, waited for hours and hours only to be told that my hormone levels were fine and that no ultrasounds were done over the weekend. I was sent home thinking that everything was going to be fine. The next day, I started to sense that something actually could be wrong. I called the maternity ward again and specifically requested an ultrasound as I was too stressed about the bleeding. I was told that someone would call me on Monday to make an appointment. That's when I knew that I had to tell Rose. I didn't want to start working on Monday and then be like "By the way, I have to go to the hospital now". So, I called her and told her about everything that was going on the past few days. She was supportive and assured me that whatever I had to do regarding this matter, she had my back. The next morning, I made my way to the hospital. Unfortunately, I had to go by myself. Consequently, I had to deal with the apathy of the sonographer and the nurse alone. The sonographer didn't even have the curtesy to wrap the devastating facts that there was no heartbeat, no 10 weeks old foetus and that I was going to miscarry whatever there was any time soon in a more sensitive packaging. The nurse "kindly" advised me to stay home, take Paracetamol and only go to A&E if I faint. Great. What a heart-warming way to communicate to a woman that there wasn't going to be a baby that she had been expecting so eagerly although she had only known about it for a couple of months. The best of all is how I was basically told not to come back to the hospital unless I was fainting. I was left alone to experience a miscarriage at my very own home without any medical supervision and professional mental support. Just great. I'm going to spare you the bloody details of the whole experience and jump to the end result. I didn't have a baby anymore, I was traumatised and every corner of my own house reminded me of the incident, I hated the NHS (National Health Service) more than ever before, and my feeling of not wanting to be in that country was as strong as ever. Last but not least, I remember having decided for myself that a second child maybe was just not meant for me. Could the start to a new year be more terrible? I guess it could, but for me, it was as terrible as it could get. I was praying to see the purpose behind the pain I was going through, soon. And I did.

12. Freedom

The Decision

Family members who had known about the pregnancy and consequently the miscarriage called to express their sympathies and to cheer me up. Obviously, in such a situation, although everyone meant well, nothing really helped and I didn't want to hear any of it. One thing, however, stuck to my mind. One of my second degree cousins, who is also my husband's elder brother's wife, said to me: "Have your next baby in Germany." This was meant to be a joke on the side and clearly a bunch of other things were said during our conversation, but the above sentence triggered me. Whether I was going to have another child or not was secondary. My primary thoughts were around the idea of moving back to Germany. What was I still doing in this country? Who was I kidding? I didn't like living there one bit. This incident put everything into perspective and here comes my long strain of thoughts that repeated itself over and over again in a different order, with the same outcome: The job I was in didn't fulfil me and it wasn't the job that I've always wanted to do, my husband and I barely saw each other as we always worked so hard in order to make ends meet, yet the money was always tight at the end of the month and we were never able to afford things like holidays or just stuff that we'd like to have, the healthcare system, to put it in nice words, was not the best, I didn't like being in my own house anymore because of what had happened and how the NHS handled things, our son would have to undergo the same school system that I condemned and didn't want to work in anymore, BREXIT, ... I'm going to stop here as it feels like I could go on forever. The point is that I didn't see myself carrying on like this; not just me, but us as a family, we couldn't go on like this. I had nagged my husband many times about going back to Germany before our son was born. Understandably, he had many doubts about that plan and we used to get into fights because of that topic. So, eventually, I just dropped it and tried to find ways to settle, mentally and physically, where I was. But now I felt like this was my call to try again. I wanted to suggest this idea one last time to my husband. So, I mustered up all my motivation and strength and did it. Up to that point, he used to just brush it off and change the topic whenever I had brought it up. This time it was different. He actually heard me out. I told him about all the things that I thought would be better in my eyes and said if the language is the only problem standing in the way, it's an easy problem to solve. I was so convinced that not knowing the language should not be the decisive factor keeping us from this step. I had researched and found out that he wouldn't even need to pass a language test beforehand in order to immigrate with his spouse and child, both German citizens. Nevertheless, I left the decision entirely up to my husband. I promised him and myself that if he said no, I would never ask him again, but if he said yes, that I wouldn't ask him anything ever again and take care of everything from the move to finding jobs and settling down. To my gigantic surprise, I didn't have to ask him again, because he actually said yes. He was fed up with the way we were living our lives, too and wanted a fresh start. I for one couldn't believe what I had heard. After several years of pretending to be happy with where I was, I finally got the chance to start over with my family and create a better life together. I double-checked multiple times whether my husband was really serious and when he made clear to me that he was, I drafted a plan for our very own "BREXIT".

Project "BREXIT"

This undertaking consisted of many steps and I'd like to think that it was and always will be the most nerve-wrecking project of my life. So much was on stake and we didn't know if we were going to make this plan work in our favour. There were so many questions and although we had my family waiting for us and who had promised their support, we were scared. I was positive that things would work out, but I was scared that it would take years and years for us to make a come-back after the move. The house sale was the most stressful part of the whole move. Although we had found a buyer within 24 hours of going live with the advert through an agency, the process itself dragged for several months. At the same time, I was looking for a job. My husband said that it was best that I find an employment first as I am the citizen and it would be easier for me. I was hoping that, in case I couldn't find one before we moved, my company would allow me to continue my work from Germany. This meant that I had to talk to Rose and tell her about the decision we had made as a family. So far, I had only spoken to my friend Kiana, who also encouraged me to go for the position at the company, about this. My husband had told his family and I had told mine. We had informed our neighbours as they would see the for sale sign outside our house anyway. We decided not to tell anyone else until closer to the time we actually moved. And we didn't know when that would be. The plan was to have made it to the other side by the end of the year but it was hard to predict since everything was still fresh and new. So when Rose asked me if I knew when I was going to quit (it was not possible to work from Germany due to contract and income tax laws), I didn't have an answer. You should know that I hate it when things are up in the air and I can't plan ahead. I find it very difficult to deal with although I have become much better at it. Nevertheless, I like it when things are set in stone and I know where I'm going and when I need to do what. Since my company wouldn't let me work remotely from Germany, I knew I had to find a new job. At least that was certain and so the job-hunt started all over again. I had hoped that I wouldn't have to do that again for a few years, but what the heck, for the sake of finding my feet in Germany I was happy to do it again. Ideally, I wanted to work as a teacher. It was clear to me that I'd be able to work and survive in the German education system. It's by far not perfect, but I'd like to think that things have been going much better for teachers. I remembered having great experiences as an intern at different schools during my undergraduate. Additionally, a friend of mine, who teaches at a Gymnasium (the equivalent of a grammar school) and whom I got to know in the very first week of university in Germany told me how her days were filled with work and at the same time how rewarding the work was. She said that the students give you something in return for all the work you do for them and the parents are grateful. Furthermore, the admin work does not take the upper hand, but your main job is to actually teach the children in front of you. So, for me it was out of question that I wanted to go back to teaching when we moved to Germany, at least at some point. I didn't want to sit around and wait for an opportunity to come along. So, I contacted one of my teachers, Mr. Peter, who was still teaching at my hometown Gymnasium. He started off by being my ethics teacher when I was in Year 5. A couple of years later, he became my class and English teacher. And eventually, he taught my ethics class again when I was in Year 12 and 13. So, he was one of the teachers who probably knew me very well and someone who was always interested in what was going in his students' lives. I had met him at my brother's graduation and he wanted to know how life was and how teaching was in England.

Obviously, I just gave him a snippet of what my life was like, but my point is that he is the kind of person who cares. I thought it might be a good idea to contact him and find out what the teacher employment situation was like in Germany. I sent him an email asking if he thought I'd have any chance of finding a teaching position at a Gymnasium with my qualifications and experience. His response met my expectations. I knew that it was difficult, virtually impossible to find a job at a Gymnasium without having completed a Masters of Education and the 15 months long teacher training, but like the Germans say: "Asking doesn't cost anything." Mr Peter said that with a little bit of luck I might be able to score a position at a different type of school (in Germany, there a different types of schools for different ability levels) a Realschule, Hauptschule or Berufschule, for instance. According to him, my subjects, English and French, were in demand and my language and work experience was impeccable. Yet, the Germans want to see certificates. Without even having to ask, he explained that there was no use in asking for a teaching post at his, i.e. at my old school since they were over-staffed already and there was no sign of anyone leaving any time soon. It didn't look good on the getting-back-to-teaching front, but I didn't feel like giving up and there were other jobs out there that I could do. I had applied to a couple of language learning centres and one of them got back to me, proposing a meeting once I would have arrived in Germany. I had also applied for a customer service job at an online furniture store. It was a work-from-home job which meant that we wouldn't have the stress of finding a place for ourselves until we actually got there. I could have worked from my parents' place where we wanted to arrive and establish our "base point" anyway. I had passed the initial exam and was invited for a virtual interview, which went well, too. I was just waiting for a response from their recruiter. While I was waiting, a much more interesting opportunity popped up on my phone on a Thursday morning. I had updated my LinkedIn profile and my notification settings to suit my new needs right after we had decided to move. When I woke up and took my phone to switch off the alarm, I couldn't believe what I saw. I put on my glasses and I realised that I had read correctly in the first place. A Rudolf Steiner school in Germany, to be more precise in the city where I did my undergraduate, was looking for a French and English teacher to start in the upcoming term. The best part was that career changers were welcome. It meant that, since this school (and all Rudolf Steiner schools in Germany for that matter) is not run by the government but belongs to the private education sector, I didn't necessarily need the full German teaching qualification for this position. The school can choose to hire someone who hasn't completed the German state school teacher training. The hired person would have to attend seminars for Waldorf teaching in order to immerse in the pedagogy and develop teaching methods and strategies that suit this type of schooling. I figured that this very unexpected opportunity was my best and one and only chance to get back into teaching in Germany. So, I whipped up the best CV of my life.

A New Life

I don't want to bore you with unnecessary details about the move from the UK to Germany as it was an extremely stressful undertaking and cost, at least for me, every drop of energy.

There were a few complications that needed sorting out and the house sale didn't go through until we had already moved and had been living in Germany for almost a month. What's probably more interesting is that I had landed the teaching job in Germany. For me, that was the jackpot. This place was the last city that I saw myself going back to. Not because I didn't like it, in fact, I had never wanted to leave in the first place as I liked it so much as a student. I just didn't dare dreaming about living there again. It couldn't have gone better and after all the years of battling with target grades, GCSE results, disinterest in languages, and being confined to a certain syllabus and schemes of work or a certain way of teaching, I finally found a place where I could be myself and even more. Rudolf Steiner schools, or as they are called in Germany "Waldorfschule", follow the anthroposophy as a core belief and principle. For teaching and learning it means that whatever subject you teach, the content needs to reach the students through different channels and most importantly it has to appeal to their emotions and soul. Rudolf Steiner was convinced that whatever you do or learn that is far from what you can relate to, will not stick to your mind and is torture. The school and the school day are structured different from the state schools (Rudolf Steiner schools are private institutions). For instance, all classes from year one up to year 13 are under the same roof. The main subjects are taught in so-called epochs, which means that one subject is taught intensively for a few weeks and then concluded with an epoch test. After that, a new epoch starts. The students aren't given any grades until year nine, when the upper school begins, and receive annual descriptive reports in which every teacher explains in much detail how they have perceived the student in lessons. If you want to know more about Waldorf teaching, I recommend you visit any Rudolf Steiner school website or the one of Germany's Waldorf school trust (Bund der Freien Waldorfschulen). I'm in my second year of teaching there now and I haven't had a single day on which I wanted to quit teaching again. I have stopped counting days until the next holidays and I am free to teach whatever I think is suitable and needed in my classes. I can be as creative as I want with my teaching and I have made myself a name as the teacher who organises fun English theatre plays and inspiring French excursions. The majority of the parents is on my side and some even keep motivating and telling me how grateful they are for my work. Apart from one exception, I haven't had a parent who tried to blame me for their child's behaviour or a colleague who wanted to tell me how to do my job and even those parents are on my side now. Observations are meant as opportunities for learning from each other rather than catching the colleague making mistakes, because there must be something on the observation form. There is no observation form! The children don't need to be entertained with a smartboard presentation every lesson on every single day. In fact, using the smart board or any media for teaching is not allowed until middle school. Lessons are meant to be creative, the students are supposed to get moving and do stuff instead of sitting on their chairs and staring at a board for 45 minutes. I can decide when and how I want to set a test and I am not carrying home a pile of tests or books on a regular basis. I was able to connect with the children in one way or the other, regardless of whether they liked English or French as a subject. Although there are days where I'd rather stay at home, (but who doesn't have those?) I get all enthusiastic once I'm in the classroom. I'm very aware that it is different in other schools and in other cities. The students might not be as nice as in my school, the workload is significantly higher at a Gymnasium where I wanted to work before moving to England and the parent community can depend on the area as well. Every school has its strengths and weaknesses as well as every education system. What I can say though is that the education system in Germany is different and suits me better. Whether it is better than the English one is disputable, but I'm finally able to say that I love what I'm doing for a living and that I can identify myself with it. This Rudolf Steiner school has given me the opportunity to rediscover myself and my professional self in ways that I didn't even know were possible. I'm appreciated and given the opportunity to become the teacher that I didn't know I wanted to be but now think I cannot not be. I have finally found my calling, not as a teacher for Gymnasium as I wanted to when I was a university student, but as a Waldorf teacher. It's funny and interesting how the routes you take and the paths you choose lead you to a destination eventually, but what's more important is what you take with you along the journey. I for one can say that looking back, I'm glad that I had to go through those unpleasant years of teaching Modern Foreign Languages in English schools that have shaped me as a teacher and as a person. The experience I have gained in my darkest moments as a teacher has made me the teacher and person I am today. I'm now combining the wisdom of two worlds and make it a version that suits me and the children in front of me. When it gets a little more stressful these days or when colleagues complain about the students or the amount of work they have to complete, I remind myself of my days as a teacher in England and I just smile. I have overcome one of the biggest mountains and now I am exploring and enjoying the beautiful valley that lies behind it. I have won professional freedom and therefore personal fulfilment as I'm a teacher at heart. For me, it is not just a job, but my calling and my life's purpose (apart from being a wife and a mother). I thank my husband for giving me the greatest gift of trusting me and allowing me to do what I'm doing now and those family members and friends who supported me in reaching for this freedom. I would like to stress again that the criticism and disapproval I expressed in this book are subjective and based on personal experiences. My message is that every teacher should look into their heart and soul and consider whether what, how and where they're teaching resonates with their inner self. After all, teaching is an art, a very personal profession, not even a profession, but a calling, at least for me and for those who believe it.

13. Priceless information

In this chapter, I will retrospectively address some of the key information that I would have benefitted from before continuing on the teaching path in England. It would have spared me a lot of physical and mental stress, anger, frustration and unhappiness. But I like to see it as factors that showed me what I didn't want in life and helped me to get to know myself a great deal better.

The Attitude

"I can speak English, I don't need to learn French", "Miss, why do I we have to learn German?", "I'm not going anywhere, so why do I need to learn all this", "I don't care about French and my mum doesn't either", and so on and so forth. These are just a few examples of student comments that were thrown at me in the past few years when trying to teach languages or when explaining why languages are so valuable in English schools. "I love passing on knowledge and my love for languages to children and young adults" I used to say in interviews. However, this has proven to be a much greater challenge than I would have ever imagined in my worst nightmares. During my studies, my several school placements, and my times as a private tutor in Germany, I always considered myself to be an inspiring teacher, whose passion and interest for languages seemed contagious. The children wanted to be good in at least one foreign language. It was only after I started working in school in England that I realised that the predisposition of having an interest in another language is not common in England due to the fact that "everybody in the world speaks English". Obviously, it would be unfair and racist to generalise British people's attitude, however, I've heard English people say about themselves that they're terrible at languages. I also heard parents saying to their children "Oh this is just the languages room; we don't need to stop here" when they passed the MFL display room at an open evening at school. There was a point in my career when I realised that I was not teaching these children languages. I was selling them languages, I was entertaining them by planning lessons with games and sweets as a reward for behaving well and participating, and if there was a group of students who wanted to do well, I was teaching them how to pass the exam. I had heard countless times from teachers of other subjects that they didn't envy my job having to teach languages to a population that doesn't see the need or the value in them. In my very last position as a teacher of German and French, my frustration reached its climax when I stood in front of a class of around 25 students day-in, day-out and none of them remembered what I covered in previous lessons, despite the fact that vocabulary and grammar were drilled and practised and written down. Hardly any student could be bothered to move a finger, flip back a page in their exercise book and find the answer to my questions. I can't put into words how discouraging and demoralising it was for me having to teach the same things over and over again for weeks, only for the students to come back after the weekend or half-term holidays and say that they didn't know, because they don't speak the language, or shout out random French or German words that they remembered for some reason but didn't make any sense in that particular context. It seemed as if they didn't want to remember anything or didn't see the need to remember anything even if they were highly capable. A consequence of the common disengagement and disinterest is misbehaviour, low-level disruption, and sometimes disrespect. Now, in order to manage that, one has to be a "tough cookie", which leads me to my next point.

Behaviour Management

This is the key word; behaviour management is THE term in the world of teaching. No lesson can be delivered without some sort of behaviour management, which is at the heart of teaching.

However, if you want to achieve anything, not only in your lesson, but in your career as a teacher in England, the key is to learn as many behaviour management strategies as possible. Apart from knives and flying chairs, I have seen everything in my five years of teaching in England, and I used to ask myself: "Why are these children so disrespectful to me? Why are they behaving in a way that disrupts the lesson and holds everyone back from learning?" I could not find an answer back then and I will not find an answer at any time, because I now know that for all these years, I was living a lie. I had the illusion that all children would be like I used to be as a child and student. When I decided to become a teacher and when I was studying, I never considered the fact that there would be all kinds of children. Children who are kind and hard-working, children who are kind but lazy, children who are rude and disruptive, children with difficult family backgrounds and so on and so forth. And of course, most kids will not be able to separate whatever is going on at home from their school life. Children are not a blank page when they come to school and I cannot expect from them to just sit there and learn. In addition to that comes the attitude I touched upon in the previous section and that seems to be instilled into most British kids in one way or another. All I can say from experience is that you have to establish your authority, learn how to be an entertainer and actor, and sell your subject before anything else. You have to earn the students' attention even before starting to actually teach your subject, deliver successful lessons, hence be a successful teacher, flourish in your profession, and at the same time enjoy it. This does not mean that I had successfully mastered behaviour management; I was far away from being perfect and unfortunately, I have had enough of having to put on a show so that the students would pay attention to me. As a matter of fact, I think that no teacher will ever be perfect as every student is different, every cohort is different, and every generation is different. Each teacher will encounter at least one student or a class in their career that will require their whole repertoire of behaviour management strategies. I understood this when I was talking to colleagues, who have been teaching for years and were struggling with a certain class or student.

If you want to be a teacher in England, the first thing you have to develop is a thick skin and a repertoire of behaviour management strategies. In addition to that, you should learn to take yourself less seriously. Why am I saying this? The reason is that only if you distance yourself from your self-respect, your dignity, your ego, you will prevent those three from being damaged. You will prevent yourself from feeling useless and unaccomplished after a tiring day at school, where either a student disrespects you, the work you do or your subject that you have such a huge passion for or where you felt like you can't cope with the amount of work. You will prevent yourself from taking all that mental stress home and letting it out on your family or starting to dislike yourself. In my view, it is the hardest thing to do, to take yourself less seriously. Especially, coming from a cultural background in which respect for the older person, whether you like or dislike that person, is preached day-in and day-out and having grown up in a society and educational system in which almost all responsibility and accountability for academic success and progress lies with the student and the parents, I have found it extremely challenging, if not impossible, to accept that a child half my age has just insulted me or denied my authority. Yet, I am expected to engage in a restorative conversation with that exact same child where I, as the adult, and as the educated and highly-qualified person, have to pander to the child who has sworn at me or disrupted my lesson. And then there is the education system that just seems to demand every drop of energy you have.

The System

"The British school system is designed to punish the teacher and not the student" is what a non-teaching colleague of mine once said. The sad part is that I had to agree with him.

The cause for this is deeply rooted in the education system. The pressure that is applied at the very top, ripples through to the bottom of its hierarchy. I feel that education is seen as a business in many ways and this has an impact on everyone who is concerned. If you drive around in the towns of England and you get passed a school, any school, whether primary or secondary, or even a nursery, you will see banners advertising the institution's recent Ofsted rating. It will say "Outstanding" or "Good" because these are the two best ratings that an educational institution run by the state can get. There are two things that I find disturbing about this matter. Firstly, that schools are rated and secondly, that they are being advertised. The school's rating is, amongst other factors, based on the teachers' performance. Some schools "just" monitor a teacher's progression whereas other schools rate the teacher on the same four-point scale as Ofsted judge the school itself. In my experience the following can happen: In the first scenario, where the teacher is being monitored, the head of department or line manager of the department could come into several lessons and see whether the teacher is adhering to certain standards and whether there seems to be any progress in terms of teaching and learning. The other approach where the teacher is rated, I experienced as follows: The rating is dependent on one single lesson in a term that is observed by a senior member of staff. They observe the efficacy of the teaching and learning happening in that lesson as well as the amount of feedback that the students receive from the teacher in order to improve their learning. How can one single lesson out of many determine a teacher's efficacy or ability to do their job well? There could be several reasons as to why that person is not performing well on that very day of the so-called performance management observation. And why does a teacher have to "perform" at all? You see, the salary increment is also dependent on the students' grades. At least this was the case at my last school in England. If all students in your GCSE class obtained what they got for their target grade, you earned more in the following term. If not, you had to wait for a general adjustment to teachers' salary by the government. I just can't understand why a competitive atmosphere between colleagues is created like that. What if there are a bunch of kids who can't be bothered to work for their chosen GCSE subject and therefore, surprise, don't work for it? What if there are children whose abilities don't leave them the privilege of being picky with their GCSE choices so that they had to pick a language as the lesser evil? What if there is this one student who made it his or her mission to sabotage your lessons, just because they think it's fun? Yes, you are the teacher, yes you should have developed strategies to help your students and stay in control in your lessons, but what about the uncontrollable and unpredictable factors? Well, in the English school system, everything seems to be predictable, even the child's development and grades and if you don't do everything you can and more than that to ensure that these predictions turn into reality, you have lost. Not only have you lost all your time and energy, but also the chance of being seen as a good teacher. While in Germany the responsibility for academic success, but also for having the necessary school material lies with the student and the parents, in England the teacher and the school seem to be accountable for both. How it usually works with the academic success, I have explained just a few lines above, but what do schools and teachers have to do with exercise books, scissors, pens and glue sticks? When I was a child, my parents received a list of books and other material they had to purchase for me for the next term. I went to the bookshop and the stationery shop or the supermarket with my parents a couple of weeks before the new term started and collected the text books we had ordered in advance and bought all the necessary material. This was the common procedure to prepare for the upcoming school year and it was a fantastic time, too! All the shops would have loads of stationery on sale and the variety of everything made the whole experience even more fun. Call me a geek, but I used to (and still do) love stationery. In Germany, you will see every child up until roughly year five with a huge satchel, specially designed to hold the textbooks and all the other supplies and ergonomically fit the child's statue. Usually from year six onwards the kids find themselves too cool for that kind of backpack and get themselves a different bag or rucksack. Yet, they would still carry the books and stationery with them in that bag. Obviously, there is the exemplary student who brings everything that is needed to every lesson and then there is the student who forgets half the stuff at home, but you get the gist. In England, it seems that generally exercise books, scissors, glue sticks and sometimes even pens are supplied in school. If you forgot your pencil case at home, you could get by on the school's supply of stationery. On top of that, many schools don't work with text books, but provide the students with the necessary pages as photocopies or the teachers distribute the books in class if needed in that lesson. Students would sometimes even come without anything useful in their bag, (or even come without a bag), because they knew they would get the stuff in school. They kept losing their exercise books and didn't bother finding it, because they knew they'd get a new one in school. Or, what I find even worse, they treat their exercise book in a manner that it is not recognisable as such. Pages would be ripped, missing or skipped for no reason. And guess who was made responsible for ensuring that those exercise books stayed somewhat decent? If you didn't have glue sticks in your classroom, all the worksheets you hand out won't be stuck in, because hardly anyone would have their own glue stick in their pencil case. Will you believe me if I tell you that at two of my schools, the budget was too low for classroom supplies that I ended up buying glue sticks for my classes only to find the glue be smeared on the tables or the floor or to be thrown at each other? I watched my hard-earned money go to waste. Again, I'm being a little over the top here. I bought a bunch of glue sticks in the pound shop or ordered a bulk off the Internet, but why on Earth should I buy the stationery that is supposed to be provided by the school, in my eyes bought by the parents or students themselves, out of my own pocket and then put up with it being destroyed and misused? Additionally, it takes up almost ten minutes of the lesson to distribute and collect back glue sticks and even more if you have to give out new exercise books as well. There were countless lessons in which I stood there counting the glue sticks I got back at the end and waiting for one or two to be returned. Sometimes I had to threaten the students with losing their break time if that one glue stick didn't appear right now. What a fun way to end a lesson! And then in department meetings, your head of department would point out that since we're working on a low budget and have to wait until the next delivery of supplies comes along, we must ensure that glue sticks are returned, that we cut and trim the worksheets in advance for the students so that they are stuck in without having to use a whole page, that the kids make use of every little space available in their exercise books, and treat it in an acceptable way. Could it get any more infuriating? Yes, it can! Sometimes, I found myself (and colleagues) sitting there, gluing sheets in or fixing a bunch of exercise books for the students, because it needed to be done and nobody wanted the kids' bad exercise bookkeeping to reflect negatively on the department. Because you see, bad exercise bookkeeping by the student means bad teaching by the teacher... I understand that the system is just trying to look out for children and to avoid them having to carry too much weight around. But in my eyes, what those kids are taught by how it's done in most schools right now is that they don't need to take responsibility over their material, hence their education. For me, going to school doesn't only mean learning maths, history, English, geography or German. It means learning values such as responsibility over your actions and belongings.

Yet, what I have seen in my time as a teacher in England is that bottom-line everything seems to be about progress and outcomes and if the progress or outcome is not the desired one, the fault must lie with the teacher. Although oftentimes it is alleged that the curriculum is designed to help the children develop their personality and learn for life, in my eyes, it doesn't reflect what's actually happening. It might be true that the curriculum is multi-faceted, with a lot of activities and opportunities to learn and appreciate life values, however, at the end of the day, the aim seems to be always the same: good numerical outcomes. If students or teachers suffer from stress and anxiety along the way it is noticed, but the root cause doesn't seem to be addressed. Most schools have a support system in place for the more vulnerable children and the ones who have a hard time keeping up with the workload and being a child at the same time, but I wonder: Has anyone ever asked themselves why so many children seem to have mental health problems at such a young age? Children these days have a lot to put up with, due to social media and an overload of fast-moving information. An exam marathon halfway through or at the end of the school year can't be good for them. The fact that four-year-olds are put into school when they are meant to run around, have fun, and enjoy their careless lives doesn't help at all. By the time they reach secondary school, they have undergone hours of sitting in one spot at school and at home while doing homework, preparing for their SATs (standardised tests to assess the children's educational progress in primary school) and attending after school programmes that are supposed to enhance basics such as maths and reading. They would have missed a significant amount of time being JUST children. No wonder that one half is sick and tired of school when they reach puberty and the other half doesn't know a life beyond school where real-life skills are required. I'm exaggerating here, in order to make a point. And the teachers? Already in primary school the workload is unrealistic. I spoke to a few primary school teachers during my career and the lament was always the same: too much work, not enough money, no time for a life outside of school. For the older and more experienced colleagues it seems less tough, I would say. They have done their lessons over and over again with thousands of students and no one dares to question their expertise and know-how. Consequently, they're not asked, or let me say, not pushed to adapt their lessons according to the changing standards of the school or the department. But how do young teachers stay in their profession? A colleague who had also worked in English schools once said the following: "They try to land a leadership position so that their teaching hours decrease and they have people to do certain jobs for them. That way they have to deal less with the daily struggles of a classroom teacher" and I'm going to add that thus, they have the power of micro-managing staff members. I don't think that everyone necessarily micro-manages on purpose or out of their own will. I believe that a pressurising system, and I mean any system, is the root cause for micro-management. Let's take the education system in England. If there was no Ofsted that rated schools based on a teacher's "performance", which again is dependent on the students' grades, why would anyone with a leadership position have to micromanage anyone? As I said before, the pressure that is applied at the very top causes a chain reaction. Each staff member pressurises someone below them in the hierarchy because their superior wants to see results. As far as I'm concerned, the actual result beyond the numbers is: stressed teachers and anxious students. I just wonder: is anyone truly happy like that? If you ask young teachers, they'd probably say that it's not great but they wouldn't know what else to do and the money is good. Or they might say that it is just the way it is, which isn't great, but there is nothing you could do about it. They even might say that they do it all for the kids. I wonder if they're really happy in their jobs, though. Maybe they are. It is interesting to see that the government is throwing money at people who want to become teachers. There is a considerable amount of funding promised to those who take up a teaching course. The profession with the teaching scholarship is even advertised on TV and in the radio. Most teachers seem to leave the profession within the first five years. But is money really the problem? Can the issues I have described be solved with money? Do 25.000 Pounds funding make up for all the frustration, stress, anxiety, self-doubt, and sacrificing your time? Doesn't the cause for the lack of teachers lie somewhere else? I am not saying that not a single teacher in England is happy with what they're doing. Certainly, there are many teachers who love their profession. I'm just saying that I for one didn't and would never get the kick out of investing every minute of my short life, without having a work-life-balance, into the students' grades and making them pass or excel at their GCSEs and A-Levels. I'd like to say that I want to be a person first and invest in myself. Yes, teaching is my calling and my life's purpose, but I as an individual come first. How am I supposed to work effectively and with the same enthusiasm for decades if there is hardly any time to recharge and do what's best for myself? And when it comes to my job, I want to invest my working life into accompanying children while they become responsible adults with the skills to go out into the world and face life with its ups and downs; adults who seek fulfilment through intrinsic motivation rather than chasing an extrinsically motivated goal; adults who have learned for the sake of learning and not in order to pass an exam. After all, I think school is not just about the factual knowledge and the numerical results. School is about making sitting there for the most part of your day worth the while through memorable moments, learning from one another and mutual respect and appreciation. It's about having unforgettable lessons because they were inspiring, funny or true-to-life. Good grades and well-founded factual knowledge should be a by-product of those lessons, but, in my eyes, not the main intention. Maybe this is happening for other teachers in other lessons and it just never happened for me while teaching in England. However, I am of the opinion that, and I'm sure many would agree, the education system is inviting everyone who is concerned to focus on the result rather than on the journey. My journey as a teacher in England was set out to have an early end right from the beginning due to many reasons. I won't blame anyone or anything; I won't blame a colleague, not a school, not an incident, not the system for the end of my teaching career in England. All I can say is that I probably wasn't the right person for that job in that country after all. Having always been a very non-rebellious pupil, teenager and adult, I had and still have my difficulties understanding misbehaviour. And being someone who is just used to a different mentality and different views on education, I found it hard to blend into the English education system and work in it. Nevertheless, I want to stress that I learned a lot during my years as a teacher in England. As I previously said I am now combining the good stuff from both "worlds". I have learned how to be tough but warm towards pupils, how to manage my time and organise myself, how to communicate effectively with parents and that I am a survivor. I have developed a tolerance for stress and pressure that will always serve me in tricky situations in my life. So, after all, I wouldn't have become the person and teacher I am today, if I hadn't gone through all the stuff I've told you about in this book. Yet I am glad to be back where the views on education and the teaching profession are compatible with mine.

Epilogue

Teaching, for me, is not about filling empty jars and showing how to pass exams, but about awakening curiosity and the love for learning. It's about showing young people how learning in itself is an accomplishment and that one day they will be ready to master their life's tasks and not the ones set by their teachers. Finally, a teacher is not someone who just teaches something mechanically, by doing exactly what the colleagues do. Teachers are artists, who share not only knowledge but also wisdom. And they do it in a way that suits their personality, because that's how it is done best and therefore the act of teaching can't and shouldn't be standardised. This is why I didn't fit into the English school system; and I'm glad that I didn't.

I encourage everyone to do what's best for them. After all, you can't pour from an empty jug. If you don't wholeheartedly identify with what you do, it won't benefit anyone, not you, nor the ones you work with. Ask yourselves if you really want to keep doing what you're doing, where and the way you're doing it for the rest of your lives. If the answer is 'no', don't be afraid to take a step back, regroup and make a new plan. Life is too short to be stuck in a job that doesn't fulfil you, especially since work is the place where we spend a third of our lives. Don't be afraid of the detours along the way and don't regret the dark moments. They're all part of the best version of yourself that you are yet to become. Feel free to take my journey as an example for finding professional happiness and fulfilment. Thank you for taking the time to read my personal story and maybe you were able to take something from it.

Printed in Great Britain
by Amazon